GLOBAL SOCIAL PROBLEMS

GLOBAL SOCIAL PROBLEMS

Allan Mazur

Rowman & Littlefield Publishers, Inc.
Lanham • Boulder • New York • Toronto • Plymouth, UK

ROWMAN & LITTLEFIELD PUBLISHERS, INC.

Published in the United States of America
by Rowman & Littlefield Publishers, Inc.
A wholly owned subsidary of The Rowman & Littlefield Publishing Group,
Inc.
4501 Forbes Boulevard, Suite 200, Lanham, Maryland 20706
www.rowmanlittlefield.com

Estover Road
Plymouth PL6 7PY
United Kingdom

British Library Cataloguing in Publication Information Available

Library of Congress Cataloging-in-Publication Data

Mazur, Allan.
   Global social problems / Allan Mazur.
     p. cm.
   Includes bibliographical references and index.
   ISBN-13: 978-0-7425-4803-9 (cloth : alk. paper)
   ISBN-10: 0-7425-4803-1 (cloth : alk. paper)
   ISBN-13: 978-0-7425-4804-6 (pbk. : alk. paper)
   ISBN-10: 0-7425-4804-X (pbk. : alk. paper)
   1. Social problems. 2. Social history. 3. War and society. 4. Human
ecology. I. Title.
HN28.M39 2007
361.1—dc22   2006037988

Printed in the United States of America

♾™ The paper used in this publication meets the minimum requirements of
American National Standard for Information Sciences—Permanence of Paper
for Printed Library Materials, ANSI/NISO Z39.48-1992.

For Rachel and John, and Julie and Matt,
and their world.

Contents

Acknowledgments

I know of no one person who is an expert on all of the topics covered in this book. Therefore, I am grateful to the diverse specialists, and some nonspecialists, who commented on one or more of the chapters. Those who were most helpful are Cissie Fairchilds, Michael Freedman, Craig Humphrey, Jerry Jacobs, Robert Jensen, Louis Kriesberg, W. Henry Lambright, Robert Lerner, William Mangin, Polly Mazur, Denton Morrison, John Nagle, Thomas Neumann, Joseph Nye, Eugene Rosa, Mark Rupert, Seymour Sachs, Harvey Sapolsky, Stuart Thorson, and George Zito. I thank John Olson for constructing maps used in this book.

1

Objectivity and Bias

Principle 1: The Rashomon Effect

In the classic Japanese movie *Rashomon*, a samurai and his wife are traveling through the forest when they are confronted by a bandit who kills the man and has sex with the woman. After a woodcutter finds the samurai's body, the bandit is arrested and brought to trial where each participant relates the incident from his or her own viewpoint (Kurosawa, 1950).

The bandit admits that he was struck by the lady's beauty and decided to take her. To that end, he captured the samurai and tied him to a tree. Then he overpowered the lady, whose fierce struggle changed to passion as she finally gave herself willingly to the bandit. Afterward the lady, now disgraced in the eyes of two men, told the bandit that either he or her husband must die, and she would belong to whoever killed the other. The bandit untied the samurai and, after a heroic fight, finished him with a sword thrust, but by this time the lady had fled.

In the lady's version, the bandit raped her, and afterward she lay weeping in front of her trussed-up husband. She looked to him in her grief, but the samurai stared coldly back with unmoving eyes, driving her to frenzy. "Kill me if you must," she cried, "but don't look at me like that." She staggered toward him with a dagger to cut his ropes, but as he continued his blameful

1

gaze, her desperation grew until she fainted. On awakening, she saw her husband, still tied to the tree, the dagger in his chest.

Now the court hears the testimony of the dead husband, who talks through the voice of a spirit medium. The samurai-medium claims that the bandit, after raping his wife, tried to console her, asking her to come away with him. She agreed, per-haps because she was too ashamed to stay with her husband. But regaining her resolve, she tells the bandit, "Kill him. As long as he is alive I cannot go with you." Both men are shocked, and the bandit asks the still bound-up husband if he should kill *her*, but she runs away. In sympathy, the bandit cuts his captive's bonds. The husband wanders off listlessly and then notices the dagger on the ground. He retrieves it, raises it over his head, and plunges it into his own chest.

Which version is correct? Each participant relates the inci-dent in a way that justifies his or her own behavior while casting blame on the others. This occurs so often in real life that we speak of the "Rashomon effect" when people give inconsistent accounts of the same situation, and each account suits a position the teller wants to defend.

At first glance, the major question in Rashomon seems to be: what really happened? But the plot thickens when we learn that there was a witness. The poor woodcutter knows more than he has told, for he came upon the scene right after the bandit had his way with the lady. He heard the bandit begging for the lady's forgiveness and asking her to leave her husband and marry him. The sobbing lady cannot answer, but she finds the dagger and cuts her husband's ropes. Seeing this, the bandit says, "I under-stand. You mean that we men must decide." He draws his sword, but the husband says, "Stop! I refuse to risk my life for such a woman." The woman looks at her husband in disbelief as he tells the bandit, "If you want her, I'll give her to you." By now the bandit is having second thoughts and decides to leave, but the lady begs him to wait. Soon all three are arguing, as the lady calls both men cowards. The men fight awkwardly with swords. Finally, the bandit kills the samurai. The lady flees.

None of the participants comes out very well in this version, but is this really the true story? We are never certain because it turns out that the woodcutter too has selfish motives, for after everyone else left the scene, he took the valuable dagger and did not want the police to know. Is his story any more trustworthy than the others?

For years, cinema critics have debated whether the film's director, Akira Kurosawa, meant the woodcutter's version to be the correct story or not (Richie, 1972). In any case, the film raises a more profound question. Rather than simply inquiring what actually happened, it asks if there really is a single, uniquely correct account. If there is one true version, then any deviations from it must be lies or errors. But perhaps each person told the story as he or she really thinks it happened. In some sense, reality is in the mind of the beholder, and the reality for one person may differ from the reality for another (Jacobs, 1982).

Certainly there are limits to this relativistic view of reality. The samurai was killed with either a sword (as in the accounts of the bandit and the woodcutter) or a dagger (as told by the lady and the samurai himself). Somebody is right and somebody is wrong. In principle one could settle the point by measuring the size of the wound to see which weapon fits. But the truth is not always easy to determine, even in principle. What did the samurai really communicate when he stared at the lady? She interpreted his gaze as a look of malice and contempt. Perhaps he was staring blankly because he was in shock. If the same look meant one thing to the husband and something else to the wife, then they did indeed experience different realities. Or consider the bandit, who believed that the lady succumbed to his masculinity, giving herself willingly to him after her initial rebuff. Did she in fact "turn on" to the bandit's forcefulness, or did he play out in his own mind the common male myth that some women enjoy being raped? Of course, one can conjecture anything one likes because the story is fiction, but the same questions would apply to a real-life situation.

The Rashomon effect recurs throughout this book because social problems are always controversial, and with any proposed solution, some people stand to gain and others to lose. Anytime we find interest groups in conflict, whether the rich against the poor, or one group of nations against another, we will find inconsistent accounts of a situation, with each account serving the interests of those who subscribe to it. We must recognize when these claims represent separate realities, so that each side's position is as good as the other, and when there is a single reality, so that one side is right and the other wrong. Unless we attempt to find objective truths, we will be lost in an irresolvable morass of claims and counterclaims.

Conflicting accounts always have some points of agreement. We will assume a claim to be correct if all parties agree to it (although occasionally it turns out that everyone is wrong—a situation sometimes called "pluralistic ignorance"). In Rashomon, all agree that the samurai and his wife were traveling through the forest when they encountered the bandit, that the bandit tied up the husband and had sex with the wife, that afterward the husband and wife were estranged, and that the samurai was stabbed to death. If this were real life rather than fiction, we would assume that these points of agreement had in fact occurred.

When there are disagreements about factual matters, it is sometimes possible to find objective evidence showing who is right. As we have already discussed, it would have been possible to decide if the samurai had been killed by a sword or a dagger by measuring the size and shape of the wound. Although fingerprinting was not available in medieval Japan (and besides, too many people handled the weapons), one can imagine such kinds of evidence that would implicate one person rather than another.

Sometimes one person's opinion is as good as another. At other times it is possible to say who is correct and who is wrong. It is important to recognize both situations and to be able to distinguish one from the other.

Rashomon and 9/11

President George W. Bush has often and fairly consistently given his account of September 11 and America's subsequent "war on terrorism." An example is his address to a joint session of Congress on September 7, 2003:

> Nearly two years ago, following deadly attacks on our country, we began a systematic campaign against terrorism. These months have been a time of new responsibilities, and sacrifice, and national resolve and great progress.
>
> America and a broad coalition acted first in Afghanistan, by destroying the training camps of terror, and removing the regime that harbored al Qaeda. In a series of raids and actions around the world, nearly two-thirds of al Qaeda's known leaders have been captured or killed, and we continue on al Qaeda's trail. We have exposed terrorist front groups, seized terrorist accounts, taken new measures to protect our homeland, and uncovered sleeper cells inside the United States. And we acted in Iraq, where the former regime sponsored terror, possessed and used weapons of mass destruction, and for 12 years defied the clear demands of the United Nations Security Council. Our coalition enforced these international demands in one of the swiftest and most humane military campaigns in history.
>
> For a generation leading up to September the 11th, 2001, terrorists and their radical allies attacked innocent people in the Middle East and beyond, without facing a sustained and serious response. The terrorists became convinced that free nations were decadent and weak. And they grew bolder, believing that history was on their side. Since America put out the fires of September the 11th, and mourned our dead, and went to war, history has taken a different turn. We have carried the fight to the enemy. We are rolling back the terrorist threat to civilization, not on the fringes of its influence, but at the heart of its power . . .
>
> Two years ago, I told the Congress and the country that the war on terror would be a lengthy war, a different kind of war, fought on many fronts in many places. Iraq is now the central front. Enemies of freedom are making a desperate stand there—and there they must be defeated. This will take time and require sacrifice. Yet we will do what is necessary, we will spend what is necessary, to achieve this essential victory in the war on terror, to promote freedom and to make our own nation more secure . . .

Fellow citizens: We've been tested these past 24 months, and the dangers have not passed. Yet Americans are responding with courage and confidence. We accept the duties of our generation. We are active and resolute in our own defense. We are serving in freedom's cause—and that is the cause of all mankind.

Thank you, and may God continue to bless America.

Compare this to Osama bin Laden's account, given in a videotape broadcast shortly before President Bush's reelection and released in translation by the Arab news agency Al Jazeera on November 1, 2004:

Praise be to Allah who created the creation for his worship and commanded them to be just and permitted the wronged one to retaliate against the oppressor in kind . . .

People of America, this talk of mine is for you and concerns the ideal way to prevent another Manhattan, and deals with the war and its causes and results.

Before I begin, I say to you that security is an indispensable pillar of human life and that free men do not forfeit their security, contrary to Bush's claim that we hate freedom. If so, then let him explain to us why we don't strike for example—Sweden? And we know that freedom-haters don't possess defiant spirits like those of the nineteen [September 11th attackers]— may Allah have *mercy on them.*

No, we fight because we are free men who don't sleep under oppression. We want to restore freedom to our nation. Just as you lay waste to our nation, so shall we lay waste to yours . . .

Even though we are in the fourth year after the events of September 11th, Bush is still engaged in distortion, deception and hiding from you the real causes. And thus, the reasons are still there for a repeat of what occurred. So I shall talk to you about the story behind those events and shall tell you truthfully about the moments in which the decision was taken, for you to consider.

I say to you, Allah knows that it had never occurred to us to strike the towers. But after it became unbearable, and we witnessed the oppression and tyranny of the American/Israeli coalition against our people in Palestine and Lebanon, it came to my mind.

The events that affected my soul in a direct way started in 1982 when America permitted the Israelis to invade Lebanon and the American Sixth Fleet helped them in that. This bombardment began and many were killed and injured and others were terrorized and displaced.

I couldn't forget those moving scenes, blood and severed limbs, women and children sprawled everywhere. Houses destroyed along with their occupants and high rises demolished over their residents, rockets raining down on our home without mercy. The situation was like a crocodile meeting a helpless child, powerless except for his screams. Does the crocodile understand a conversation that doesn't include a weapon? And the whole world saw and heard but it didn't respond.

In those difficult moments many hard-to-describe ideas bubbled in my soul, but in the end they produced an intense feeling of rejection of tyranny, and gave birth to a strong resolve to punish the oppressors. And as I looked at those demolished towers in Lebanon, it entered my mind that we should punish the oppressor in kind and that we should destroy towers in America in order that they taste some of what we tasted and so that they be deterred from killing our women and children.

Following the principle of Rashomon, the two accounts are contradictory, each justifying the position of its utterer. Both men invoke the same God (called "Allah" by Muslims) as their ally.

When opponents or their supporters make contradictory factual claims, these may sometimes be deemed true or false on the basis of good evidence. Immediately after 9/11, some in the Arab-Muslim world doubted that bin Laden was behind the attacks. Instead they blamed the suicide mission on CIA or Israeli agents, who they thought acted as provocateurs. A corollary belief on the "Arab street" was that 4,000 Jews employed in the twin towers did not report for work on September 11 (Friedman, 2002). These conspiracy theories were shown unequivocally false when Osama bin Laden acknowledged his role in the attack. On the other side, President Bush justified his 2003 order to invade Iraq by asserting that Saddam Hussein had weapons of mass destruction and was working cooperatively with bin Laden's terror network. These charges were also shown to be incorrect (Select Committee on Intelligence, 2006).

Many other contradictory claims cannot be objectively decided, even in principle. When adversaries differ on value judgments, on religious or political ideologies, these are subjective matters and are not amenable to empirical evaluation. Who is the true "freedom fighter," George Bush or Osama bin Laden? To most readers of this book, and certainly to this author, bin Laden's posture and actions are indefensible. Still, we must try to understand his and other perspectives if we are to deal justly with the diverse peoples of the world. Conflicts involving beliefs about religion and other deeply held values are usually not logically resolvable. Ultimate Truth lies in the eye of the beholder. Whose side is God truly on?

Sometimes time heals these differences. In 1988, Libyan leader Moammar Gadhafi's agents planted a portable radio filled with explosives on Pan Am Flight 103, bringing down the plane with 259 people aboard, including 35 students from my own university. The world condemned Gadhafi, and the United Nations placed sanctions on Libya. Suffering from this isolation, Gadhafi eventually renounced terrorism, paid reparations to Flight 103 families, and gave up his attempt to develop nuclear weapons. Declaring this turnaround a triumph of his tough foreign policies, President George W. Bush approved the lifting of sanctions and the return of American oil companies to Libya. Very soon, my morning newspaper reported, "Sitting in a tent surrounded by camels and goats, [then] Prime Minister Paul Martin [of Canada] found common ground with Moammar Gadhafi on Sunday in celebrating the Libyan strongman's one-year anniversary of his renunciation of weapons of mass destruction" (*Syracuse Post-Standard*, December 21, 2004). Martin and Gadhafi were pictured shaking hands and smiling broadly. In 2006 the United States restored full diplomatic relations with Libya. Perhaps in twenty years Osama bin Laden will be welcomed as a guest in the White House.

Principle 2: Coalescing around Group Identities

Osama bin Laden draws much support in Arab and other Muslim regions of the world, even in nations whose leaders are strongly allied to the United States like Saudi Arabia and Jordan. There we see in operation a second important principle: People coalesce around group identities, supporting "their" side in a conflict.

Group identity is the tendency to sympathize more with members of one's own collectivity (whether a family, a community, a formal organization, a religious or ethnic group, or a nation) than with individuals outside that collectivity. Spectator sports demonstrate the ease with which we identify with "our" team, being joyful at its victories and sorrowful at its defeats. In a more serious arena, most citizens rally in support of their nation and its leader during hostilities against foreigners.

Members of minority ethnic groups often share a sense of identification, vis-à-vis the majority, even when they are personally unacquainted. Furthermore, polarization increases as stressful conflict increases. Of course there are exceptions. Some Jews support the Palestinians against the Israelis, and some Arabs support Israel, but the general tendency is clear enough.

The most fervent followers of Osama bin Laden hate Americans indiscriminately. They do not differentiate American civilians from American soldiers—all are fair targets. Sadly, some Americans lump all Muslims together too; they cannot distinguish the Arabs of al Qaeda from other Arabs, or even from Muslims living in the United States. A nationwide Cornell University poll conducted in 2004 found that 44 percent of Americans agreed that the U.S. government should restrict in some degree the civil liberties for Muslim-Americans. Highly religious respondents supported restrictions on Muslim-Americans more strongly. This is distressingly reminiscent of public acquiescence during World War II to our government's incarceration of Japanese-Americans in concentration camps for no reason other than their Japanese ancestry.

Ask your friends what distinguishes Arabs from other Muslims, or Sunnis from Shiites, and you may find they have no idea. Yet these group identities are intensely important in today's world, sometimes differentiating warring parties. Examples: The nineteen attackers on 9/11 were Sunni Arabs, fifteen of them from Saudi Arabia. The nation of Iraq is bitterly divided among three competing ethnic groups: Shiite Arabs (the majority), Sunni Arabs (favored under the regime of Saddam Hussein), and Kurds, the smallest group, who are Sunni Muslims but not Arabs.

We see in global conflict a persistent linkage between group identity and the Rashomon effect. Rather than a single samurai or a single bandit adopting self-justifying accounts, we encounter entire nations or other collectivities that more or less accept such accounts. Often these become the rationale for jihad—holy war— or for any other kind of war.

Plan of the Book

The following three chapters provide historical background to discussions of current global problems, which are taken up in subsequent chapters. These early chapters explain how the globe came to be divided by the major social boundaries that exist today. Starting with the ancient roots of separate European and Asian urban-cultural areas, we examine the development of industrialization in the nineteenth century. Taking World War II and the collapse of the Soviet Union as the two great pivot points of the twentieth century, we examine the Soviet-American confrontation, the end of the Cold War, and the emergence of the United States as the sole superpower.

Chapter 2 covers 2 million years of human existence, with special emphasis on the transition of human society from its early hunter-gatherer phase to agrarian civilization. Chapter 3 examines the nineteenth-century industrialization that separated the rich nations from the still poor agrarian nations. Chapter 4 focuses on changes since World War I. With this background, we take up specific global problems, which are described here in overview.

Chapter 5 is about war. The ultimate catastrophe would be full-scale nuclear war, and happily its likelihood is at least temporarily diminished since the end of the Cold War, but we also look at conventional warfare and terrorist activity.

In chapter 6 we consider the extent of inequality around the world, both in material lifestyle and in human rights. Which areas of the Third World are in the worst shape, which are improving?

While the populations of most industrialized countries are fairly stable or declining, those of most developing countries are growing rapidly. With population growth comes urban congestion, especially as squatters move to such "primate cities" of the Third World as Mexico City, one of the largest and least manageable urban areas on earth. While China has taken severe measures to limit population, at times restricting families to only one child, Catholic countries of Latin America officially discourage modern forms of birth control. The problems and prospects for population in these various cultures are discussed in chapter 7.

We often think of "scarcity" as having too little food, oil, or other resources for too many people. Just as important, perhaps more so, is the problem of distribution of resources to the people who need them. Often in African famine areas, food already on-site does not reach the people who are starving. Why do American farmers, who could feed so much of the world, limit the amount of food that they produce? Many scarce resources would be more plentiful if we were willing to exploit the environment to get them. Energy is an obvious example, for there is plenty of coal if we want to dig it out, spread it around, and burn it up—but that would be destructive to the landscape, would be dirty, would pollute air and water, and would alter the world's climate. Technology may be the key to solving these problems, allowing us to use fewer resources in cleaner, healthier ways. Technology has improved birth control techniques and given us the "Green Revolution," which enables previously food-poor countries like India to become exporters of agricultural produce. On the other hand, it creates the weapons of war and the tools for industrial exploitation, and in so doing may create worse problems than it solves. Chapter 8 considers the interplay of technology, resources, and the environment.

Finally, after looking at so many problems, chapter 9 is about solutions. Everyone wants a livable world safe from warfare. Americans, in addition, favor civil liberties over totalitarianism, and democracy over monarchy or theocracy. What feasible means are available for achieving these goals, and what are the prospects that they will succeed?

2

Agrarian/Urban Transformation

People more or less human have been around for about 2 million of the Earth's 4.5 billion years.

A *billion* is too large a number to grasp easily in our minds, but it is worth trying. Someone living a billion seconds would be over thirty years old. It may help to think of the total span of the Earth's existence—4.5 billion years—as being compressed into one calendar year with the Earth cooling into a solid sphere in January. Judging from fossils, which can be dated, the first microscopic life appeared in March or April, but it was not until November that fish with backbones swam in the oceans. Dinosaurs flourished and then died off in the middle weeks of December, to be replaced at about Christmastime by mammals as the dominant land animals.

Some of these mammals were the early primates, whose main features were their grasping hands (rather than claws) and eyes at the front of their heads (rather than the side) for stereoscopic vision, adaptations well suited to a life of climbing through trees. In the week between Christmas and New Year's Day, some of the primitive primates evolved into monkeys (by December 27), and some monkeys evolved into early apes, the ancestors of present day gorillas and chimpanzees (about December 29). Some of the early apes were our own ancestors, their descendants eventually becoming enough like us—more human than apelike—to call them members of our own biological genus, *Homo*. This was about 2 million years ago or, in our compressed time scale, after supper on New Year's Eve. Fully human people, members of our own species, *Homo sapiens*, appear by ten minutes to twelve, and with the invention of writing, all of recorded history fits into the minute before midnight!

The Start of Cultural Change

Every human society has a culture, which is a set of things that you learn while participating in that society which you would not necessarily learn in some other society. The culture includes a language, social customs and rituals, technological know-how, food preferences, and so on. It was once thought that culture was a strictly human phenomenon, but field studies of some nonhuman primates show that they too have cultures—very simple ones—that are passed from one generation to another, as when young chimpanzees learn from adults how to strip and shape weeds, insert these into termite holes so that the insects crawl on the weeds, fish them out, and eat them. Of course, human cultures are much more complicated than those of any nonhuman primate, especially in our use of language. The essence of human culture, however, is not just its complexity but also its astounding variability. People and their customs are different the world over. The people of most societies eat cooked meat, but some societies eat no meat while other people eat raw meat, and a few people eat other people. The cultures of human societies vary not only from one to another, but within any society the culture changes from generation to generation.

Of the "almost human" species to appear around 2 million years ago, *Homo erectus* was the most widespread throughout the Old World and is probably our direct ancestor. As one might expect, the culture of *Homo erectus* was more complex than that of any ape but less so than that of full humans. They used fire, constructed dwellings with hearth places, and practiced organized big-game hunting. They made a fairly standard tool kit that is called "Acheulean" (after a French site where early examples were found), which included stone choppers, scrapers, awls, hammerstones, and a characteristic two-faced hand axe that is the hallmark of the kit. The most striking and "unhuman" thing about the Acheulean tool culture is its constancy; hand axes that have been found at sites widely separated in distance and across a million years of *Homo erectus*'s existence, look similar to one another (Johanson and Edey, 1981). The culture of *Homo erectus* was remarkably static.

By roughly 100,000 years ago—quite recently on our time scale—*Homo erectus* was replaced by people sufficiently like us to call them *Homo sapiens*—members of our own species. By 50,000 years ago, these people looked so much like us that if they were dressed in current clothing, they could go unnoticed in a crowd (Simons, 1989). The culture of *Homo sapiens* was richer and more variable than that of *Homo erectus*. Well-made tools appear not only in stone but also bone, antler, and ivory. Artifacts are engraved with geometric or naturalistic designs. There is sewn clothing—sometimes with bead decorations, projectile weapons, clay figurines, and cave paintings that are awesome even by modern standards. The pace of change took off as never before, producing different cultures from place to place and time to time (Pfeifer, 1982).

Since the articulation and transmission of cultures is closely tied to language, it is tempting to guess—it is only a guess—that these modern-looking people had linguistic abilities far beyond anyone who had preceded them. With their appearance, the stage was set for more rapid and profound cultural change than had ever occurred before.

Population Dispersal

By 10,000 years ago, humans had spread from their apparent place of origin in Africa to nearly all of the habitable areas of Eurasia. People had reached Australia and had begun but not yet completed the colonization of the Pacific islands of Oceania.

They had crossed an ancient land bridge from Siberia to Alaska (exposed when the sea level dropped as water was frozen into huge glaciers), moving down into North America and then South America. Thus, virtually all of the world that is populated today was populated then, although at much lower densities.

During these migrations, which may have moved only a few miles per generation, travelers encountered certain physical barriers that were especially hard to cross, like wide stretches of ocean and arctic terrain. It is remarkable that people managed to reach islands in the far Pacific and to enter North America near the Arctic Circle. We suppose that those who completed these crossings were few in number, and that having arrived in more easily habitable environs they became the "founders" of populations that would settle these new areas. No doubt, destinations as big as Australia or the Americas received successive waves of immigration, but it seems likely that the number of people crossing over difficult physical barriers was small compared to the number who were born in the new area. In such cases, the founders—the first arrivals—were especially influential both in setting the physical features of the people who would live in the area and in forming their culture.

It is apparent from a physical map of the world that there are several major zones, each bounded by formidable physical barriers such that land travel is much easier within zones than between them. Australia is an obvious example, being a large island, and the same is nearly true for North and South America. East Asia is separated from west Asia by arctic tundra, the Gobi Desert, and the high Himalayas. The vast Sahara Desert separates the Mediterranean basin from southern Africa.

After humans settled these various zones, their populations expanded in relative isolation within the physical barriers. As a result, the language and cultural forms within each zone and the physical characteristics of its people became somewhat individualized. Some of these unique features must derive from the original features of the founder populations who settled the zones, whereas others must be long-term adaptations to local conditions, but it is difficult to say which is which. Are northern Europeans light skinned because light-skinned people were the first to migrate into that cloudy environment, thus becoming the ancestors of a light-skinned race? Or, of all those born in the area, were people with light skin better able to produce vitamin D under the scant sunlight, giving them some survival advantage over dark-skinned people, thus leaving more light-skinned descendants? No one knows.

As European sailors began their long voyages of the fifteenth century, reaching the Americas, Africa, India, and the Orient, they encountered people who looked and acted differently than themselves. It was natural to assume that the exotic behaviors of these foreign races were as inborn as the color of their skin or the shape of their eyes, and such impressions remain the basis of modern racism. With the hindsight of four centuries, we have a better understanding of racial differences. Members of all races easily interbreed, producing healthy and fertile offspring, demonstrating that we all belong to the same species. We know, too, that all recognizable physical differences between races are relatively superficial features such as coloring, hair patterns, variations in physique, and differing distributions of blood types and genetic diseases. Furthermore, individuals and subgroups within any major race differ among themselves at least as much as the average differences between races. Indeed, it is difficult to know where the boundary of any single race might be drawn, since there are always people who could as easily be sorted into one as another (Mazur and Robertson, 1972).

More importantly, we now know that the behaviors associated with each race are learned features of their culture, not innate to their biology. The grandchildren of eastern European serfs, Japanese farmers, or African tribesmen, transported to an American setting, all learn English as well and with the same accent as children of any other ancestry who grow up in the same neighborhood. Given the benefits of a middle-class rearing and good nutrition, representatives of each race have written fine literature, produced modern art, earned Ph.D.s, and become wealthy in business. While there are marked inequalities among the races in these accomplishments, they appear in all cases to be explainable as the results of different opportunities and barriers that confront each race.

Two Transformations

Lacking any written record older than 5,000 years, we must depend on other traces to reconstruct most of the history of modern people. One of the best available indicators of social change is the changing size of the world's population. Archaeologists have determined both the regions of the Earth that were inhabited at various times and their approximate population densities, so it is possible to draw a rough picture of the changing size of the world population over the past 50,000 years. The most familiar feature of this picture is the dramatic increase of population within the past 400 years, an explosive growth in the number of people, which now stands at over 6 billion.

To mark "6 billion" on a graph of world population and still fit it on the page, we need to represent billions of people with a few inches of the vertical axis. As a result, any changes during earlier periods of history, when world population was far below a billion, do not show up, and we get the mistaken impression of a nearly constant population until 400 years ago. In fact, there have been major fluctuations in world population throughout history—the most famous being the loss of one-third of Europe's people from the Black Death in the fourteenth century. Beginning about 10,000 years ago, there was an unusually strong and persistent period of population growth, which in important ways was similar to the one we are experiencing today (Deevey, 1960). Of course, our contemporary population explosion is unprecedented in size and rapidity of growth, but the same could be said for the earlier period of growth, compared to what had preceded it. Both population surges—400 years ago and 10,000 years ago—mark fundamental social transformations, probably the two most important cultural changes in human history.

Why did population increase so rapidly in these two periods? No one really knows, but a full explanation would certainly encompass other social changes that accompanied population growth and were intimately involved with it. Ten thousand years ago, the human population lived as hunters, scavengers, and gatherers, as they had for all prior human history, finding their sustenance where chance provided it. They were probably nomadic, moving in small bands to follow food sources. During seasons when food and water were especially abundant, bands may have gathered together into larger tribes for trading, to socialize and find mates, and for ritual purposes, as is common among hunting and gathering societies today.

Then, as humans increased in number, they increasingly grew their own food by planting crops and raising animals. Some growers remained nomadic, but others aggregated into settled communities, raising their food in nearby fields. One might suppose that communities grew because there was a more plentiful and dependable food supply than before, but it makes as much sense to argue the reverse: that communities produced more food because they had more mouths to feed. It is a chicken and egg problem. The exact sequence is less important than our recognition that at that time human society—at least much of it—began a fundamental change, from wandering hunters and gatherers to agriculturalists living in settled communities. We will call this the "Agrarian/Urban Transformation."

The more recent period of change, within the past 400 years, is often associated with revolutions, especially the Industrial Revolution, the French Revolution and other political revolts against traditional aristocracy, and the "revolution of rising expectations" in the Third World. We will call this complex of changes the "Industrial Transformation" to emphasize its most important feature—the aggregation of workers into very large and technologically efficient industrial organizations controlled by corporate and governmental bureaucracies.

Writing was invented during the Agrarian/Urban Transformation, and it was soon followed by written history, which often focuses our attention on local events that seem important to the writer in his time—perhaps the exploits of kings or the travels of explorers. The tendency of later historians is to cluster these local events into themes of broader significance, for example, showing us that the ostensibly separate actions of various kings during a particular period were all part of a general rise of absolutist monarchy, or that the movements of separate explorers had the collective effect of opening up the New World to Europe. In the same vein, we may step back even further to recognize the overwhelming significance of the two transformations in shaping our modern world.

As recently as 10,000 years ago—only 400 generations back—the world's people lived in small societies as collectors and hunters. Then, within a few thousand years, life in several places was transformed into an agrarian mode, settled in permanent communities supported by nearby fields of grain and by animal husbandry. The animals became sources of power and transport as well as of food. The populations of growing cities became differentiated into separate classes, one better off than another, with some form of king or ruler holding control, partly through hereditary right and partly through the strength of military alliances. Cultures grew, merged, diffused, and diversified. Never before was there such a profound change in the human condition. Even the Renaissance, the Reformation, and the rise and fall of the Roman Empire are minor events compared to the Agrarian/Urban Transformation. Only the Industrial Transformation compares in importance.

The Beginning of Civilization

This new agrarian life was the base upon which civilization emerged over the next 5,000 years. By "civilization," I mean an advanced form of agrarian society that usually has writing, calendars, astronomical observation, mathematics, monumental architecture, planned ceremonial and religious centers, specialization in arts and crafts, metallurgy, and intensive irrigation projects. In one of the most remarkable coincidences of history, the emergence of agrarian civilization occurred not once but in at least six places at nearly the same time: Mesopotamia, Egypt, India, China, Mexico, and Peru.

The coincidence is striking enough without exaggerating it. When we say that these civilizations appeared at "the same time," we do not mean within five years of one another but rather within 5,000 years. Still, considering that nothing like this had occurred during the prior tens of thousands of years since the first appearance of *Homo sapiens*, not to mention 2 million years of other species of *Homo*, then the timing is very close. Nor did the transformation at any one place occur within a single generation but more like 100 generations, although again, relative to what had come before, this was fast. Nor was the development of agrarian civilization limited to these six places, but these are the best known and probably the earliest in their respective parts of the world. These six seem to have developed rather independently of one another.

Mesopotamia

Although it is difficult to pinpoint beginnings, the earliest of these civilizations apparently began in the "Fertile Crescent" of the Middle East, an arc formed by the eastern coast of the Mediterranean Sea and the Tigris and Euphrates rivers, and named for its easy cultivability compared to the arid regions nearby. Near the present-day city of Jericho, located on an oasis close to the eastern border of Israel, archeologists have uncovered the ruins of biblical Jericho. It is one of the earliest-known "cities" with one of the longest records of human habitation. Its ancient inhabitants, over generations, repeatedly constructed new buildings on top of old ones, forming a large mound or tell. By digging deeper into the tell, one digs backward in time.

The lowest level, dated at 10,000 years ago, is a hunting and gathering site with flint tools and the remains of a small building. At a little higher (and later) level, from 9,000 years ago, are the remains of one of the first settlements based on irrigation farming of grain and legumes. Meat was still supplied by hunting, in this case the wild gazelle, rather than from domestic animals. The town was composed of round houses constructed from mud brick. It covered an area equivalent to one square city block (one-eighth mile on a side), surrounded—at least in part—by a defensive wall of stone, 6 feet thick, to which a stone tower was attached, 30 feet high and 28 feet in diameter with an inner staircase leading to the top of the wall.

Following the destruction of this town, a new one was built on its ruins about 8,500 years ago and again enclosed by a stone wall. The houses were now rectangular, with polished plaster floors colored red or yellow. Several structures may have served as public buildings or temples. Although pottery had not yet appeared at Jericho, there were sculptured heads modeled in clay with shells inset for eyes. Tool finds such as sickle blades, mortars, and pestles are consistent with an agrarian lifestyle. The goat, apparently including a domesticated form, replaced the wild gazelle as the main meat source.

Pottery appeared in Jericho less than 7,000 years ago and bronze about 2,000 years later. The city walls were destroyed and repaired many times in this interval, and Jericho was sometimes deserted, its population changing repeatedly. By 4,000 years ago, the city was again prosperous, its fortifications consisting of a huge sloped wall of beaten earth supported at its base by a stone retaining wall 20 feet high. Many tombs found outside the city contain alabaster and bronze, scarabs and jewelry, wooden objects, reed mats, and baskets. The city was probably destroyed again, but it was inhabited in the thirteenth century BC when Joshua reputedly led the Israelite invasion of Canaan; however, there are no signs of "tumbled-down" walls from that period (Avigad, 1974).

Towns developed into city-states in Mesopotamia, as the alluvial plain between the Tigris and Euphrates rivers is called, especially in the region named Sumer, near the head of the Persian Gulf. The location was good for agriculture, watered by rivers whose spring flooding brought fresh nutrients to the soil, although the distribution of water had to be managed through irrigation. Perhaps the need for irrigation encouraged farmers to join together in the cooperative maintenance of water channels. No doubt the value of land varied depending on its access to water, and this inequality may have encouraged the emergence of classes of people who were better or worse off.

The typical Sumerian city-state was a collection of residences, shops, and public buildings, encircled by a wall and surrounding agricultural fields. Of central importance were the stepped temples (ziggurats) that would become the typical form of Babylonian monumental architecture. These temples were concerned not only with religion but with the collection and distribution of agricultural surplus and craft products as well. The

Sumerians maintained trade routes over hundreds of miles, judging by the dispersion of objects from their sites of manufacture to distant parts of the region; and their cities were large, some covering a square mile. The first known written documents appear in Sumer 5,000 years ago, and by that time the buildings, grave sites, and the distribution of luxury goods all point to a society stratified by wealth.

Marvelous successes in deciphering ancient writing (Doblhoffer, 1973), added to the representational art that appears at the same time, enhance our ability to envision Sumerian society. The earliest documents are often concerned with routine business matters, such as receipts for cattle or wheat, and they show a numerical system based on sixty (as opposed to our decimal system). There are references to kinglike figures and to such specialized occupations as carpenter and smith. By 4,000 years ago, as the Sumerian form of city-state spread throughout the Fertile Crescent, there are accounts of hereditary dynasties, wars, and the formation of small empires. In the next thousand years, Mesopotamian cultures developed advanced art, metallurgy, legal systems, epic myths, a calendar, mathematics, trade, and warfare. One more millennium sees the rise and fall of the powerful empires of Assyria, Babylon, and Persia and brings us to the beginning of the Christian era.

Other "Pristine States"

In Egypt, less than a thousand miles from the Fertile Crescent although separated by desert, civilization appeared again along the Nile River. Agriculture developed there about 7,000 years ago, lagging behind Mesopotamia. But then Egypt surged ahead and was first to form an extensive empire by unifying the small kingdoms along the Nile under a succession of dynasties. The power and wealth of the Egyptian pharaohs are suggested by their great pyramids, in place 1,500 years before the Assyrian Empire and unsurpassed as conspicuous consumption until our own era.

Farther east, civilization rose in another alluvial valley, along the Indus River of India. Agriculture developed here, as in

Egypt, by 7,000 years ago. By 5,000 years ago, Indus society had walled cities with citadels, housing 25,000–30,000 inhabitants with copper-bronze metallurgy, standardized weights and measures, writing, binary and decimal arithmetic, and elements of religion that can be matched to modern Hinduism. In another thousand years, this civilization would disappear for reasons unknown.

The Yellow River of China provided alluvial soil for another agrarian transformation, one that moved slower than those in western Asia. Still, by 3,500 years ago a full civilization had emerged under the Shang Dynasty, displaying a building project as labor intensive as any in the ancient world: a city wall 2,385 feet long, 60 feet wide, and 30 feet high, estimated to have required 180,000 labor-years to complete (Strayer and Gatzke, 1984). Perhaps it was a precursor of the Great Wall of China, still a thousand years in the future.

Many other civilizations have appeared, but those already mentioned are presently regarded as the "pristine states" of the Old World, having developed indigenously without major elements being transported from elsewhere. To these must be added the newer pristine states of Mexico and Peru. These six empires appear to have been major sources from which civilized culture spread throughout the world, whether via trade, conquest, or example. It is likely that many peripheral areas were transforming on their own when they were overtaken by these core areas and were hastened on their way.

There is a temptation to oversimplify matters by assuming that each transformation was an invariant sequence repeated in place after place. In fact, there are differences among the core areas that are as striking as their similarities. The pristine states of Asia all occur in major river valleys, which is not true of America. Egypt was much less urbanized than Mesopotamia. The appearance of any one cultural element is variable, for example, the use of animals and the wheel for transportation was important in the Old World civilizations but not in America; metallurgy has appeared in some precivilized cultures but not in all civilized ones. Thus, the transformation did not take exactly the same form in each place. Nonetheless, one can hardly fail to be impressed by the degree of similarity and simultaneity that did occur or to wonder why it happened that way.

Explanations

We can never know with certainty why these changes occurred as they did, but our understanding of the Agrarian/Urban Transformation is much better than it was fifty years ago and is still improving. Hardly anyone today seeks one simple explanation, and it is generally assumed that several factors came together about 10,000 years ago—spurred by a general warming of the world's climate at that time, which melted the glaciers and raised sea levels—to accelerate existing trends toward agrarian civilization. The causal factors that seem most pertinent are of four general kinds, which we will take up in turn.

Diffusion

Leaving aside the question of why the very first agrarian community arose, there is a simple answer to why it happened in subsequent communities: they copied the first community. The archaeological record contains many instances of sites where an "advanced" culture appears abruptly, with no indication of transition from an earlier culture at that place. When the new culture shows the hallmarks (e.g., characteristic pottery designs, style of writing, the same domestic grains) of a culture known to have existed at another site in an earlier time, then one suspects that the culture was transferred from the earlier to the later one, perhaps carried by people moving to the newer site. When there are indications of a trade or conquest route between the two sites and when other sites in the area show similar changes, then we can be fairly sure that the advanced culture diffused from its place of origin to the new sites.

This pattern of evidence occurs so often in Europe and Sub-Saharan Africa that it was long thought that nearly all agrarian civilizations had diffused from one original site, probably in Mesopotamia. Even areas as far away as Peru were conjectured to have had direct contact with the Old World, perhaps via boats from Asia that drifted to the west coast of South America on prevailing ocean currents. Stylistic similarities between pottery from South America and Japan, both dated at about 3000 BC, suggested that the Peruvians had somehow learned ceramic making from the Orient.

As the early history of the ancient civilizations was filled out in more detail, it became clear that some of these advanced cultures did not appear as abruptly as had first been thought. Transitional forms of culture sometimes appeared in the ruins of earlier levels, especially in those places that we now call the pristine states. For example, in the Peruvian area, simpler ceramics have now been found in levels underlying those resembling Japanese designs, suggesting that pottery making was a local development (Morris, 1980). The diversity of the earliest crops among the pristine states—wheat and barley in western Asia, millet and rice in China, and maize in America—make it implausible that these all spread from a single center. Mesopotamian grain may well have started agriculture in Egypt 7,000 years ago, but Egypt's subsequent culture seems to have developed indigenously, judging from the extent that transitions can be traced in the record, and Egypt became a large unified empire well before that level of political development was attained in Mesopotamia.

Although the picture we have today cannot be regarded as the last word, it gives less importance to diffusion than previously thought. The extent of trade and communication in the ancient world is impressive, but it does not seem to account for the rise of civilization in so many core areas at nearly the same time. While there probably was early contact between some of the pristine states, especially among Mesopotamia, Egypt, and the Indus Valley, and between Mexico and Peru, these do not seem adequate to account for overall development in these areas. Diffusion does satisfactorily explain the flow of these developments from the various core areas to their peripheries, along the shores of the Mediterranean Sea, down the Nile into Sub-Saharan Africa, and to Japan.

Human Nature

The second kind of causal factor used to explain the Agrarian/ Urban Transformation is change in humankind itself. Was *Homo erectus* capable of inventing an agrarian culture? Considering his failure even to improve much on the Acheulean tool kit during his long residence on the planet, it seems unlikely. We assume that the improvements and diversity in cultures that accompanied the appearance of early *Homo sapiens* were in part due to his improved intellect. With the arrival of modern people about 50,000 years ago, cultural styles blossomed, leading us to conjecture that these people were the first to possess our level of language ability. In some sense, the unique capabilities of our species—our human nature—must have been a necessary condition for the rise of agriculture, which appeared "only" 40,000 years after our arrival. Of course, one can argue the other side: since it took that long, human nature is insufficient to explain the transformation, and other factors must apply.

To speak of human nature is a touchy matter, often connoting sexist biases. For instance, we persistently see the power of ancient civilizations residing in kingships rather than queenships, suggesting some natural tendency for males rather than females to head communities—notwithstanding an occasional matriarch. Some biological basis seems likely for this male leadership, which exists in nearly all cultural settings as well as among nonhuman primates; however, it may be nothing more than the greater size and strength of men, giving them an advantage as warriors. If that is the explanation, it immediately follows that men lose their biological advantage when community power is no longer based on physical strength, which is presumably true of modern society. Although men might still rule by tradition, there would be no intrinsic reason to regard them as more appropriate than women to lead contemporary societies.

The tendency to favor one's dependent children is part of human nature, and it makes good evolutionary sense, for parents without this regard would leave few offspring in succeeding generations. There is an emotional mechanism at work here, acting through the affection and identity that parents feel for their children, which intensifies the more they interact with one another. If the children are happy, then usually the parents are happy; if the children suffer, then the parents suffer vicariously. That is why parents take special pains to ensure the well-being of their offspring, and it likely explains the reliable presence of hereditary dynasties—the passage of power to one's children—not only in ancient societies but in nearly all societies until recently, when cultural forces have overcome this natural tendency.

We feel special concern not only for our children but for friends and close relatives too. Humans have an emotional tendency to like and identify with anyone with whom we interact positively, whether genetically related or not. (Perhaps this is a generalization of our evolved tendency to favor our children, a simple spillover to the other people with whom we interact closely.) This tendency is reflected in the most basic political behavior. It explains why families and colleagues form cliques for self-interest, especially as the population of a community grows to the point where many people are strangers to one another. It explains why my brother and I will set aside our own argument to coalesce against a neighbor who threatens one of us, and why we and the neighbor will set aside that dispute to join forces against a foreign community. If one community captures another, it explains why the winners hold themselves separate as a group from the losers, taking the losers' wealth and forming an incipient class system. All of these features of political behavior would be expected to occur in any human society with a population exceeding the size where everyone knows everyone else personally.

Language, the substratum of human culture, is almost certainly explainable as a biological trait of our species, for speaking is as natural as walking in the growth of a child. While the words of any language are arbitrary, differing completely from the words of another language with different historical roots, some semantic detail seems predetermined by our biology. Consider the following results from a study of basic color terms in ninety-eight languages representing a wide variety of linguistic stocks (Berlin and Kay, 1969).

1. All languages contain terms for white and black.
2. If a language contains more than two color terms, it contains red.
3. If a language contains four terms, then it contains either green or yellow but not both.
4. If a language contains five terms, then it contains both green and yellow.
5. If a language contains more than five terms, then it has all of the above terms plus blue.

The order of inclusion of color terms is white and black, red, green or yellow, and blue. What explains the striking consistency of this pattern? Why should red be more common than brown (the color of wood, sand, and many soils) or gray (dusk, clouds)? There are vegetated environments where a term for green does not appear and desert environments where it does.

The solution apparently lies in the physical structure of our eye. The human retina contains two types of light receptor cells: rods and cones. Rods are more sensitive than cones to light, but they recognize no colors, only variations between white and black. There are three kinds of cones, each maximally sensitive to either red, blue, or green light, with red cones the most sensitive and blue the least (Gregory, 1966). If we use this degree of sensitivity as an ordering principle, then the prime colors associated with rods and cones are ranked white and black, red, green, and blue. We have missed yellow, which has no special cone and remains unexplained. Otherwise, the physiology of the eye accounts for the ordering of color terms in language. We might expect a similar pattern of language terms for taste, since the taste buds of our tongue are tuned to sweet, sour, salt, and bitter; however, this has not been tested.

Environmental Biasing

People learn from their environments, and to the extent to which all humans experience their environments in the same way, different societies can learn similar things. Thus, from common experience, every human group recognizes that men and women are different classes of people, that babies come only from women, and that women have a special role in nurturing infants. This bias toward common responses to similar environments is the third factor explaining the independent development of civilization in different areas of the globe.

The sun is the most salient object in the physical environment of anyone living on the Earth. Any human society would be concerned with the sun and its obvious characteristics, including the color yellow—the one color term not explained by rods and cones—as well as by its circular shape, its warmth, and its cyclic coming and going, bringing light and darkness. It is nearly inevitable that people all over would mark time by the coming of the dawn or the darkness—something like a day. It is nearly as likely that people would see the changing phases of the moon as another natural time period, calculating it at about thirty days (actually 29.5), the approximate length of the menstrual cycle. People would be aware that the lunar month was shorter than the cycle of changing seasons, whether the alternation of rainy and dry spells near the equator or the movement from summer through winter and back to summer in the temperate zones.

People living in the temperate zones (but not on the equator) would notice that winter days are shorter than summer days (which is why winter is cooler than summer). Today we know this occurs because the Earth's orbit around the sun is tilted at an angle of 23.5 degrees from the plane of the equator. In winter, when the Earth is near the "top" of its orbit, the Northern Hemisphere is more in shadow than in light. Therefore, as the Earth makes its daily rotation on its axis, a winter observer in the north spends more time in shadow than in light. The shortest day of the year (December 21 in the Northern Hemisphere) occurs when the Earth reaches the highest point in its orbit. This is the "winter solstice," which was often marked by a special festival among ancient people and seems to be the basis for setting Christmas in December, since no one knows the exact date of Christ's birthday. Similarly, the summer solstice occurs on the longest day of the year (about June 21) when the Earth is at the very bottom of its orbit. These significant events were well known to ancient peoples, as they would be to anyone who routinely watched the sky.

In every society that reached the stage of civilization, people knew that the year, the cycle of seasons, was about 365 days. (Some calendars used for ritual purposes are based on other counts, for example, the 260-day year of the Aztecs or the 354-day Moslem year, but astronomers of each civilization were aware of the 365-day cycle that correlated with the seasons. On the equator, two cycles of rainy and dry seasons make up one year.) This seems an amazing feat to modern people who do not often watch the sun rise and set on the horizon, but to a people who have that luxury, it is a simple matter to calculate the number of days in a year. The sun rises (and sets) at a slightly different point on the horizon every day, which is easily marked by such landmarks as a distant peak. This point moves northward as the date approaches the summer solstice, reaching its northernmost point on the date of the summer solstice. Right afterward, the point of sunset moves southward again, reaching its southernmost point at the winter solstice. To calculate the length of a year, all one need do is count the days it takes for the rising sun to return to one of these extreme points, which is about 365 (Aveni, 1989).

We have gone into some detail here to illustrate how probable, if not inevitable, it is that any people who could both see the sky and count into the hundreds would arrive at a calendar based on days, months, and a 365-day cycle of seasons. A civilization with specialized astronomers would be carried further along this path, for example, recognizing that the year is actually about a quarter day longer than 365 days, and confronting the problem that 30-day months do not divide evenly into 365.

While constancy of environments can explain similarities among cultures that have developed in isolation from one another, changing environments can explain cultural changes. Earth's climate warmed about 10,000 years ago, just preceding the rise of agriculture. Large glaciers that covered parts of Eurasia melted, increasing atmospheric humidity and therefore rainfall. The sea level rose, flooding shorelines, but the receding glaciers opened land to habitation. These changes affected local growing conditions and must have influenced the size and movement of human and animal populations. As a result of climate change, certain plants became more widely available, including the large-seeded annual grasses that were the ancestors of wheat and barley, providing convenient seed stocks for early planters.

The pristine states of the Old World, but not of the New, arose along great rivers whose spring floods provided fresh nutrients to the soil as well as a convenient water source that could be managed by irrigation. Variations in these local environments no doubt affected development in each area. The Nile gave the Egyptians some advantages over the Mesopotamians, its spring flooding more regular and dependable than that of the Tigris and Euphrates. Also, whereas the Mesopotamian plain was open to invasion from all sides, and there were frequent incursions, the Nile Valley was protected on the east and west by desert, being exposed only from the north and south. Thus, invasions were less frequent and could be dealt with by a unified army. Furthermore, since the Nile's fertile strip was rarely more than 10 miles wide, communities were strung out along the river and therefore easy to control. Probably because of this linear dispersion of the population and their little need for defensive walls, the Egyptians never aggregated into cities as large as those of the Fertile Crescent.

One Thing Leads to Another

How did people first sail to islands over the horizon too far away for their existence to be known? Imagine a primitive community that had not yet invented boats but lived near a warm ocean coast. We may assume that its people go into the water to fish, play, bathe, or cool off, and that this is an accustomed part of their lives. Given enough years and enough floating branches or logs that children hang onto for rest or play, it seems likely that someone would intentionally put a log into the water for such purposes, and becoming accustomed to that for so many years, someone else would think to cut a hollow in the log so that they or their things might float on it more easily and remain dry. Thus boats are invented, although only for use near the coast.

As people become comfortable with their boats and develop their skills at maneuvering, voyages inevitably become longer, although always within sight of the shore. Given enough years, someone will venture out of sight of the shore but perhaps within sight of another boat that can see the shore. Some boaters move still farther away from shore, perhaps on a dare, perhaps by accident, perhaps on a divine mission, or perhaps to commit suicide. Once past the initial fear of the unknown, it is easy enough to recognize the direction homeward by the position of the sun or stars or by the prevailing wind or current or flight of birds. In any case, given enough years, there seems a natural progression from a simple society of swimmers to one of voyagers who travel beyond the sight of land. Assuming that islands are not too distant over the horizon, it is nearly inevitable that one day they will be reached, and if there is anything worthwhile there, routine traffic back and forth would soon follow.

Of course, we have no way of knowing if this sequence ever happened just this way, but something like it probably did—in many different places. The essential point is that normal people, starting out under a particular set of initial conditions, are more likely to develop their culture in some directions than others. In this case, the initial conditions are life on the coast of a warm sea and islands over the horizon but not too far; the probable outcome is island navigation. There is no predestination here or any invisible force guiding people toward some ordained goal. It is simply a matter of one's starting point influencing one's probable outcome, just as being born in 1985 rather than 1945 increases the chances that you will learn to use a computer. This is the fourth kind of explanation given for the Agrarian/Urban Transformation.

As the glaciers receded from the Northern Hemisphere's temperate zone, about 10,000 years ago, there must have been increased migration into the newly habitable areas. Groups came into contact during these movements, learning of each other's innovations and products, which provided incentives for trade. The migrations also removed people from local sources of their accustomed raw materials, forcing the abandonment of these materials unless they too could be acquired by trade. As a result, there must have been a greatly increased flow of traffic across Eurasia after the glaciers melted, consisting both of moving populations and of traders among them.

With all that traffic and trading, a tribe would have many incentives to construct a semipermanent building inhabited by a few people, even if the rest of the tribe continued as nomads. A building might serve as a trading post or market center, especially one placed at the intersection of commonly traveled roads or rivers. It might be a storage site to cache food and materials as the volume of trading goods became too great to carry, or it may have served ritual purposes—perhaps a shrine for the sacrifice of valued items to the gods. It may have been a sentry post, guarding a water hole or a good hunting site, safe from incursions by other groups traveling through. For any of these reasons, the increased pattern of trade and travel would produce an occasional building with some people assigned to it, and these in turn would become the nuclei of permanent settlements.

People wholly dependent on the natural environment for their food must have known that seeds left in moist soil would sprout. As long as someone was to stay at the building for a prolonged time, why not plant food for later harvesting? Now there was also an incentive to trap rather than kill game, for kept alive in a pen, animals would remain fresh until needed, whether for eating or trading. The penned animals could breed, saving the effort of hunting them, and their young might have been appealing as pets. In essence, here are all the features of a farm.

The people left to tend buildings may have become wealthy, especially if they were located at nodes in the developing trade networks. Their children would have shared in the good fortune and may have built houses nearby for their own families, planting more food to support the growing community. Some of these settlements grew and prospered while others failed. Those located in alluvial valleys would have special advantages, first for the natural fertility and watering of the soil, and second, for convenience to river traffic. Under these conditions "one thing led to another," and soon there were cities with social classes based on wealth, hereditary rulers, and so on.

If the Agrarian/Urban Transformation is to be explained as a natural progression from initial conditions, one naturally wonders if the same is true of our current Industrial Transformation, and if so, where will it take us? The optimist's answer is toward postindustrial prosperity and happiness. The pessimist's answer is toward a world smothered by industrial wastes or blown up by hydrogen bombs. In truth, no one will know where we are going until we get there.

Eastern and Western Cultural Zones

The interim between the Agrarian/Urban Transformation and the Industrial Transformation was eventful. In our coarse-grained analysis, these intervening events are of secondary importance, so we will skip most of them, although they constitute nearly all of recorded history! But one more question must be taken up before concluding the chapter: how was it that the separate civilizations, scattered across the Old World—not only in the pristine states but in the developing hinterlands as well—eventually coalesced into two, and later three, major cultural zones?

There was a reliable tendency for city-states to expand, through both trade and conquest. A succession of empires appeared, absorbing peripheral areas that had developed more slowly. All of them eventually fragmented, but newer empires formed to pick up the pieces, some spreading over huge territories. By 700 BC, the short-lived Assyrian Empire had encompassed all of Mesopotamia and Egypt. Also by this time, some of the peripheral areas had developed into impressive civilizations themselves, the most notable for Western culture being Greece.

In Macedonia, on the fringe of Greece (the periphery of the periphery), a twenty-year-old named Alexander ascended his assassinated father's throne in 336 BC. He died thirteen years later, having conquered nearly all of the territory from Greece and Egypt on the west, through the old empires of the Fertile Crescent and Persia to India on the east. Alexander's empire disintegrated immediately, his generals dividing it among themselves, but the adventure is important because it spread Greek culture throughout most of the conquered area.

Rome was emerging from the hinterlands west of Greece. Its expansion was slower than Alexander's, and Rome never incorporated his eastern domain, but at its height in 117 AD, the Roman Empire was enormous, encircling the Mediterranean and covering much of Europe up to Britain. As Alexander had spread Greek culture, the Romans spread their Latin descendant of Greek culture. However, being much longer lived, the Roman impression was deeper, lasting in Europe (and America) to this day, most obviously in the Romance languages (i.e., derived from Roman Latin) of French, Spanish, Portuguese, Italian, and Romanian.

Parallel events occurred on the other side of the Himalayas in China. From the modest beginnings of the Shang Dynasty, which ended about 1050 BC, came a series of expansions, especially by the Han Dynasty (206 BC–220 AD), a contemporary of the Roman Empire. In many ways, Han China was like Imperial Rome. Both expanded through armed conquest and showed impressive practical skills in administration and engineering. The Han maintained over 20,000 miles of highways radiating from the capital to the provinces, using these like the Romans' roads to control their possessions. Both empires failed at roughly the same time, partly from internal strife and partly because of incursions by less civilized tribes.

A map of some of the more successful imperial expansions illustrates the basic separation of these activities into what I call the "Western Zone" and the "Eastern Zone," separated by the Himalayan Mountains and deserts farther north. The Western Zone is immense, running from western Europe to India, including Africa above the Sahara. There is no sign here of our modern cultural and political separation of Europe from the other continents. To the contrary, the Western Zone encompasses parts of three continents, its boundaries formed by natural barriers: the Atlantic Ocean on the west, the Sahara Desert and Indian Ocean on the south, the Himalayas and deserts on the east, and subarctic regions to the north.

Obviously, it would be misleading to claim the whole region from Britain to India as a culturally homogeneous area, but in our broad view, its subregions had much in common relative to the Eastern Zone. This is best illustrated by comparing the languages of East and West. The Asian languages of the Eastern Zone are classified in the Sino-Tibetan language family, meaning that they probably evolved from one root language originating in eastern Asia. There are exceptions; for example, Japanese is a distinct language from Chinese, and so are some languages of Southeast Asia, but the overall picture of the east Asian languages shows much similarity within the broad cultural zone. Furthermore, after writing was invented in China, about 4,000 years ago, it diffused throughout the Eastern Zone, being incorporated even by the Japanese, producing the strange situation today where people from China and Japan can read some of each other's writing but cannot speak each other's language.

Most languages to the west of the Himalayas, while sounding diverse to American ears, belong to the Indo-European family, having evolved from a common root that is distinct—or at least exceedingly distant—from the Eastern Zone tongues. Besides the Romance languages, which are obviously akin, the Indo-European family includes German, English, and nearly all contemporary languages of Eastern and Western Europe, ancient Celtic from Britain, ancient Persian, and from India ancient Sanskrit, the language of the sacred Hindu religious texts. There were non-Indo-European languages spoken in this zone at the time of Rome's decline, including Semitic in parts of the Middle East. Nonetheless, the distribution of Indo-European languages, from Britain to India, shows the relatively high degree of diffusion within the immense Western Zone but not between it and China. The separation appears even more stark from a comparison of writing methods. The modern alphabet of Semitic-Greek origin appeared about 3,000 years ago, spreading to virtually all cultures of the Western Zone, although remaining quite distinct from the Chinese writing that spread throughout the Eastern Zone (Gelb, 1963).

Certainly there were contacts between these ancient zones—through trade, invasion, and religious conversion. Nomads from Central Asia, horse-mounted "barbarian hordes," periodically threatened and conquered large regions of China, India, or Europe. People in the "transition area" of eastern India and southwest Asia share elements of culture (notably Buddhism) and physical features. Still, the ancient separation of East and West was marked and quite different than the modern division. Today, we identify Europe (and America) as the West, excluding the Middle East, which has become a third major cultural zone—separate from East and West—because of the conflict between Christianity and Islam.

The Islamic religion expanded rapidly from its origins on the Arabian Peninsula, as if "bursting out of nowhere," for this desert area was as peripheral as one could get to the established civilizations. Founded by the Prophet Muhammad, who derived his teachings from both Judaism and Christianity, the movement is usually dated from 622 AD, when the prophet fled Mecca for Medina.

After Muhammad's death, the Muslims—adherents to Islam—began a string of conquests that by 750 AD exceeded the Roman Empire in size. Like Alexander's realm, it extended east to India; and like Rome, it absorbed North Africa, reaching northward into Spain. Also like these predecessors, Islam had a powerful effect on the regions it conquered, spreading not only the religion but the Arab language and its developing culture, which reached impressive heights compared to contemporary Europe.

Throughout the Middle Ages, power would shift from one party or people to another within both Christendom and Islam, but despite changing actors, the basic opposition between these two religions persisted. Each regarded the other as heathen, and their main contact was on the battlefield. The effect was to separate Europe from western Asia and North Africa, splitting the huge cultural zone that had existed since antiquity. As a result, when industrialization developed in Europe, there were no diffusion routes into Asia or Africa. America would be the beneficiary.

The Eve of Industrialization

Fourteen hundred ninety-two was a good year for Columbus. And for Spain too, which expelled the Muslim Moors—entrenched there for seven centuries—in the same year. Soon, the conquistadores would extract phenomenal wealth from the newly "discovered" Americas, destroying the empires of Peru and Mexico in the process.

Christian Europe of Columbus's time was not far advanced over some other parts of the agrarian world—economically, technologically, or aesthetically. The Forbidden City of the Chinese emperors and the Islamic world of the Moors were as grand as anything in Christendom. Even today, walking on a quiet summer afternoon by the fountains and pools of the Alhambra, the fourteenth-century Moorish palace in Granada, is as close as one is likely to come to heaven on earth. In art and architecture, wealth and invention, Europe was rivaled, if not surpassed, by the civilizations of Islam and the Orient, located in what today we regard as the less developed world.

Things would change quickly as Europe was enriched by the wealth of the Americas and as heightened trading activity encouraged technological innovation and industrialization. It is essential to appreciate the magnitude of the change that propelled agrarian Europe from a position in 1492 of relative equality with other agrarian societies in Asia and the Middle East to one of clear preeminence in the nineteenth century. By then, industrial Europe had surpassed the rest of the world not only in firepower but in wealth, science, productivity, transportation, and invention.

As the Industrial Transformation spread from Europe to America, and later to Japan, it marked out those areas of the world that we now call the advanced industrial nations. Of all the modern world's subdivisions, this is the most crucial in understanding our study of global social problems. The industrialized nations have more in common with one another than they have with the "Third World" of nations that are only beginning their industrial transformations.

3

Industrialization in Europe and America

A Martian visiting Earth in the year 1500 would have found one civilization pretty much like another. In all of them, most of the population raised crops and livestock. Cities and towns, the centers for commerce and manufacture, were interconnected by trade routes, some quite long, where land travel was by foot or animal, and sea travel was by sail or oar. Communication moved no faster than a person could. Manufacturing was carried out by individuals or small groups of people using handcraft methods, with flowing water, wind, or fire as their source of inanimate power. Large monuments and ceremonial buildings were constructed of stone, wood, and dried brick, while metal was reserved for smaller objects. Land was the most valued resource, and even the richest people rarely had large (by modern standards) amounts of spendable capital. A hereditary monarch usually stood at the top of a rigid status hierarchy, supported by a favored aristocratic class (often warriors), and at the bottom was the poorer mass of peasants. Often, one's position in this hierarchy was fixed at birth and tied to a specific piece of land, as in feudal Europe and Japan, but sometimes careerists were assigned to distant posts, as in the administrative bureaucracies of Imperial Rome or China. In either case, the rights and obligations of one rank toward another were well specified (always to the advantage of the higher ranked), and an unquestioned religion and its

41

clergy justified the existing arrangement as right and proper. Armies depended upon blades and animal power. Each civilization had impressive (by modern standards) artistic and technological achievements, and no one surpassed all the others.

If the Martian had returned in 1900, it would have seen European civilization as preeminent, followed by its direct descendant, America. No longer agrarian, these societies—and to a lesser extent Japan—had become industrial civilizations, their populations moving from farms to cities, taking jobs in manufacture and commerce. Efficient factories employing large workforces, using steam power and even electricity, produced goods in far greater quantity, and often cheaper, than ever before. Finished products were sold around the world, transported by trains and steamships that returned with raw materials to feed the factories. Steel was a common building material, and electrical communication was instantaneous. Money and industrial resources had replaced land as the most valued form of capital, with many individuals and corporations having accumulated immense amounts. Some of Europe's powerful monarchies had fallen (others would soon follow) along with special privilege for their aristocracies; America was a democracy where everyone had the same rights and obligations. Catholicism was in decline in Europe, challenged not only by Protestantism but by a secular scientific viewpoint. The technological achievements of Europe and America were unequaled elsewhere, and no agrarian army could withstand their mechanized military forces.

In less than 400 years, the industrialized societies had become separated from the agrarian ones—and not only separate but in control. This division remains the most important one in the world today. How did it happen?

Medieval Commerce and Political Consolidation

There is no simple explanation for the industrialization of Europe, but trends leading to it appear by the twelfth century during the revitalization after the "Dark Ages" that followed the collapse of Rome. At that time, Europe experienced a marked expansion of local and international commerce. Money and precious goods were the media of exchange, supplementing land as the basis of wealth. A developing class of merchants was accumulating this wealth, rivaling the power of the traditional landed aristocracy. Surplus capital became available to finance ever more ambitious trading ventures and public works, notably the awesome Gothic cathedrals of the late Middle Ages.

At the same time, monarchs began to unify—by warfare, marriage, or inheritance—the thousands of small political units that existed across the continent. This consolidation continued over the next few centuries so that by 1500 the map of Western Europe resembled its modern form, especially in the demarcation of Spain, Portugal, France, and England (Davies, 1996).

Increased commerce and political consolidation did not always occur together. Northern Italy enjoyed spectacular commercial success from the twelfth to sixteenth centuries, more than any other part of Europe, yet its major trading cities operated as separate and often hostile states. Ideally situated between Western Europe and Byzantium (the eastern remnant of the Roman Empire, centered at Constantinople), Italy's merchant fleets shuttled back and forth, trading European textiles for silks and spices sent overland to Byzantium from India and China. Italy's prosperity was further enhanced by the Crusaders, who hired its ships to transport people and supplies to the Holy Land. With this accumulation of wealth, the Italian cities vied with one another in grandeur, sponsoring the exquisite art and architecture of the Renaissance.

While Italy was developing commerce without political unification, Russia was extending its political control over a vast area without much commerce. Neither was on the road to industrialization, which usually required both elements. It was in Western Europe where political consolidation and the growth of commerce occurred together, reinforcing one another. Commercial ventures worked much better under the security and uniform law of a major king than among the uncertainties and dangers of a multitude of petty, independent barons. Reciprocally, the developing commerce with its rich merchant class gave the king a source of taxes that could be used to enforce his justice and maintain his peace. Thus, there was a natural alliance between the kings and the merchants, and an expanding commerce served both their purposes. When the Muslim Ottoman Turks captured Constantinople in 1453, shutting off the rich trade that Italy had maintained with Asia, they increased the incentive of the merchants and kings of Western Europe to find a new route to the Orient.

Voyages of Discovery

The sea routes to Asia and the Americas that Europeans discovered in the fifteenth and sixteenth centuries brought huge wealth that was invested in new trade and a general growth of commercial activity. More importantly, they led to a vast overseas system of colonies, which eventually supplied raw material for European factories and also the markets for finished goods (Hobsbawm, 1962). Ironically, the leader in overseas exploration was Portugal, one of the last nations of Europe to industrialize.

Portugal was ideally situated for voyaging into the Atlantic. Hemmed in by Spain and without a coast on the Mediterranean, there was no other option. Prince Henry the Navigator (1394–1460) made exploration a national mission, his purposes being to increase Portuguese commerce and to combat the spread of Islam (Boorstin, 1983). Bringing together mapmakers, instrument makers, and mariners, he established a major navigational school to plan the circumnavigation of Africa. Portugal became a center for shipbuilding and cartography where new bits of information were pieced together into the best current maps. Year after year, ships explored the west coast of Africa, reaching ever farther south while developing a lucrative trade in slaves, gold, and ivory. This policy eventually brought Portuguese mariners to the tip of Africa and finally, in 1497–1499, Vasco da Gama sailed around the Cape of Good Hope into the Indian Ocean, returning with a valuable cargo of spices from India. Da Gama went again to India with a military squadron, killing and looting to establish by force a Portuguese commercial empire throughout the Indian Ocean, with trading outposts eventually reaching to China and Japan. The rich Asiatic trade in spices, gems, and silks, which had come to Europe via the eastern Mediterranean and Italy, would now be transported on Portuguese ships around Africa to the Atlantic Coast of Europe.

In the meantime, Christopher Columbus was seeking a monarch to support his search for a western route to the Orient. Portugal was preoccupied with its eastern route, but Isabella of Spain, fresh from her successful expulsion of the Moors and Jews, financed the project as a means of spreading Christendom. Educated people of the time knew that the world was round and that one could conceivably reach the East by sailing west. Columbus's opponents disagreed with him primarily on the distance that would have to be sailed to reach Asia, which he put at 2,500 miles and they put at 10,000 miles. They were closer to the truth (about 13,000 miles), but of course, no one suspected that two new continents blocked the route at about the distance where Columbus expected to find Asia. He ultimately made four voyages to America (1492–1504), always insisting that he had reached the Orient, although in the end hardly anyone believed him.

More ships quickly followed the great discoverers. The Portuguese consolidated their eastward route around Africa but also sailed west to colonize Brazil. The Spanish searched for and found treasure in the New World. As it became crystal clear that America was not Asia, Columbus's plan was revitalized, for how much farther could China be? Spain sent Ferdinand Magellan to see. In 1519, Magellan set off on the greatest voyage ever, leading five ships across the Atlantic, then down the coast of South America, threading them through the excruciating strait at the bottom of the continent (which bears his name) and emerging into the Pacific Ocean. He then crossed that unknown sea, a feat taking three and one-half months (compared to five weeks for Columbus to cross the Atlantic) and finally reached the islands off Asia. While in the Philippines, Magellan became needlessly involved in an intertribal fight and was killed by natives. The one ship that was still seaworthy continued westward, rounding Africa and returning to Spain three years after it had departed, with 18 men left from the original 250, thus completing the first circumnavigation of the globe.

Effects of the Discoveries

It is doubtful that Columbus was the first European to "discover" America. Almost certainly, the Vikings reached and mapped Canada near Hudson Bay in the eleventh century. There are extensive archaeological remains from the 1500s of a Basque whaling port in Labrador, thousands of miles north of the area explored by Columbus and his followers, so perhaps these travelers from the border region of France and Spain found their rich whaling and fishing area before Columbus's landfall, without any formal announcement, keeping their find secret as protection against competition (Tuck and Grenier, 1985).

But Columbus did discover America in the important sense of thrusting it into European minds, showing that the western ocean could be crossed to find new lands with new people and that these could be conquered and controlled by Europeans. His voyages were quickly followed by Spanish conquistadores who explored and exploited the new land, slaughtering and enslaving for their own glory and enrichment, although they themselves would have said, in Rashomon style, that they were working for the glory of Spain and to spread Christianity to the heathens. Natives were pressed into service for mining silver and for plantation agriculture. Those who died under the terrible conditions were replaced by black slaves imported from Africa. Hernando Cortez wiped out the Aztec civilization with a 500-man army supplied with guns and horses, shipping its gold to Spain. Juan Pizarro looted and destroyed the Incas with a smaller force. The riches of America supported Spain throughout the sixteenth century when it was the most powerful nation of Europe.

As Spain exploited America, Portugal forcefully colonized the Indian Ocean. These two nations greatly increased the commercial activity of Europe and its concentrations of wealth, shifting the center of business activity from Italy and the Mediterranean to the Atlantic Coast. Other coastal nations, seeing the benefits of overseas possessions, were spurred into their own voyages of discovery and colonization, especially France and England, and briefly the Netherlands. The perennial warfare and shifting alliances of Europe were now extended to the distant colonies and oceans, with the result that Portugal soon lost its commercial empire in Asia to the Dutch.

The details of European politics need not concern us here, but it is worth noting the increasing stature of England, a beneficiary of the new Atlantic commerce. (Note: In 1707, England and Scotland merged into the United Kingdom of Great Britain.) The island nation of England had naturally developed as a sea power, but it lacked colonies; its first New World profits came from raiding Spanish treasure ships returning from America. This and other factors led Spain to send a mighty naval armada against England in 1588, but it was utterly destroyed by a combination of bad luck, bad planning, and superior English seamanship.

Shortly afterward, England (like France and the Netherlands) began seeking its own footholds in India and in America. The English colonies in North America did not produce gold and silver but did provide plenty of land for agricultural products that could be sent home. The English colonists in America were themselves importantly different than those from Spain, for they had come to stay, often as religious pilgrims, forming permanent and growing communities. By the middle of the eighteenth century, there were a million people of European descent in British North America, compared to 50,000 in the French sector and only 5,000 in the Spanish region (McEvedy, 1984).

The continuing European wars were (temporarily) settled in Britain's favor in about the mid-eighteenth century. As a result, Britain gained full control of the eastern third of North America. At the same time, on the other side of the world, Britain became dominant in India and emerged as the world's most powerful colonial power, a position it retained for nearly two centuries.

The Industrial Revolution in Britain

Britain's commercial role had been growing, making London the most populous city in Europe. Now its unique colonial situation, dominating both India and North America with a mighty navy and merchant fleet, was a major factor leading to its "Industrial Revolution" in the decades after 1750. The colonies served two potential functions. They were huge sources of agricultural raw material, and their large populations offered huge markets for manufactured products. All that was needed for a very rapid expansion of trade and profit was a technology that could inexpensively convert the raw material into finished goods.

The cotton textile industry was ideally suited to take advantage of this situation. Raw cotton could be shipped from the colonies to Britain where it was woven into cloth, some to be sold at home and in continental Europe, but much of it to be shipped back to America and India for sale. Cotton spinning and weaving equipment was inexpensive and was usually set up in the textile worker's home. Therefore, manufacturing capacity could be increased rapidly with relatively little capital, producing very high profits for a modest investment, as long as there was a market for the finished cloth, which there was. Between 1750 and 1769, export of British cottons increased more than ten times, mainly to the colonies (Hobsbawm, 1962). Of course, the British textile manufacturers were not a necessary link in this chain since cotton grown in the colonies might as easily have been woven there, but British policies discouraged colonial manufacture, for example, banning cotton imports from India, with the result that the English became essential middlemen.

To produce cotton textile, one first spins cotton tufts into thread and then weaves the thread into cloth. Spinning was by far the slower of these two processes and the bottleneck to increased production. With money waiting to be made, there was an acceleration of improvements in technique, many of them very clever but none requiring principles that were strange to mechanics of the time.

Traditionally, spinners worked in their own homes, in the country or in small villages. Among the most important new devices to improve the efficiency of spinning were the "water frame" and the "mule," both driven by water power and too expensive and elaborate for a cottage spinner. As a result, entrepreneurs soon went to towns where there were supplies of unskilled workers and set up factories—actually large spinning mills—with several of these machines housed together and run by a common source of power, first water and then steam. With thread being made so quickly, an increased number of hand weavers was required to convert it into cloth. But soon the weaving itself was mechanized, eliminating the need for highly skilled craftspeople. "Thereafter the weavers who had been attracted into the industry before were eliminated from it by the simple device of starvation, and replaced by women and children in the factories" (Hobsbawm, 1969: 59). The number of power looms in England rose from 2,400 in 1813 to 224,000 in 1850, as the number and size of manufacturing towns grew, like Manchester, with "hundreds of five- and six-storied factories, each with a towering chimney by its side, which exhales black coal vapour" (Hobsbawm, 1969: 56). The capitalist owners of these factories employed urban workers who were wholly dependent upon the low cash wages they earned, having no farm or cottage craft to fall back on. Factory work was specialized, repetitive, and tedious, usually requiring little skill but long hours, unlike traditional crafts and trades that varied by time of day and season and where one moved through a series of tasks in order to accomplish the worker's goals. Also, in preindustrial times there was a personal relationship between master and servant, or lord and serf, which implied rights and obligations on both sides, if unequal ones. The relationship between factory worker and employer was wholly impersonal, based solely on the exchange of wages for hours worked, a relationship that could be severed at short notice, with the employer having no responsibility for the welfare of his former employees.

Factory work was not all bad, for even the workers themselves eventually benefited from the prosperity produced by efficient mass production. Others came out much better, not only the factory owners but merchants, financiers, shippers, and tradesmen who prospered from the rapid acceleration of business. Some at the top of the heap entered the ruling class, such as the businessmen Peel and Gladstone, whose sons became prime ministers. Many more moved into the new "middle class"— below the aristocracy but above the peasants and laborers—with comfortable homes and happy families, far removed from the slums. Whereas the primary cleavage of the old system had been between the hereditary aristocracy and the peasantry, that of the industrial system was between those who had acquired wealth, or at least a comfortable living, and those who lived in virtual poverty.

Growth of Industrialization

After losing the War of American Independence, Britain could no longer prevent the establishment of textile factories in New England. Now the raw cotton from plantations in the South could be spun, woven, and brought to market without ever crossing an ocean. Industrialization in America soon rivaled that of Britain. The commercial nations of Northern Europe joined in, building their own factories and competing for the markets that had hitherto been the exclusive domain of the British. With so many nations selling textiles, demand was saturated, and opportunities lessened for high profits from rapid expansion. The first growth stage of the Industrial Revolution—based on cotton textiles—had reached its limit by 1840 when the second stage—based on coal, iron, and steel—began its spectacular takeoff.

The expanding cities required fuel, and since wood was relatively scarce in England, there was increased demand for coal, which was plentiful. Many of the deeper coal mines had water seepage, but with heightened demand driving up prices, it was worthwhile draining the mines. In 1712, Thomas Newcomen installed a primitive steam engine for this purpose. The engine was a large cylinder containing a piston. Steam, produced by boiling water with a coal fire, entered the cylinder through a valve, driving the piston upward. Then cold water was squirted into the cylinder to condense the steam, causing a vacuum so that atmospheric pressure drove the piston back down into the cylinder. By connecting the piston to a water pump, the up-and-down motion was nicely harnessed to lift water from the mine, and these engines were used widely in the coal fields.

James Watt is often credited with inventing the steam engine, but what he actually did was improve Newcomen's engine. Most importantly, Watt recognized how wasteful it was to squirt cold water into the cylinder to condense the steam, for it had to be reheated for the next stroke. His great improvement was to connect a separate condenser vessel to the cylinder, with a valve between them. In Watt's engine, like Newcomen's, steam was let into the cylinder, forcing the piston upward. But then the steam was allowed to expand from the cylinder to a separate cold condenser (by opening a valve between them), and it was there that cooling occurred, producing the vacuum that allowed the piston to fall. By this device, the cylinder stayed hot for each stroke, unlike Newcomen's engine where the cylinder was repeatedly heated and cooled. Watt's engine was much more efficient, and it could stroke rapidly (Cardwell, 1972). Soon it was replacing water power in the textile factories. By 1807, the American Robert Fulton had put one on a boat to turn the paddle wheel, and lots of people began experimenting with steam locomotives that would run on tracks.

In 1825, it made good economic sense to construct a railroad to haul coal about ten miles from inland mines to a port on the English coast. By 1850, another 6,000 miles of railways were opened in Britain, many of them not economically worthwhile in a country where most points were within easy access to water transport by sea, river, or canal. Nonetheless, investors who had accumulated capital from the textile industry, which now had limited opportunities for further growth, poured their money into railroads. In other ages, they might have spent their surplus wealth on displays of conspicuous consumption like grand palaces, but now the modern capitalist spirit encouraged the investment of surplus money to make even more money. Railroads were especially sensible for crossing vast distances of land that lacked easy water routes, such as the transcontinental route across the United States, which was completed in 1869.

The growth of rails was astounding, whether for good economic reasons or because of investment mania. In 1830, there were less than 100 miles of track in the world; by 1850, there were over 23,000 miles of track. By 1900, there were 200,000 miles of track in the United States alone. The expanding railroad demanded more coal, iron, steel, and engines. Each of these became the basis of its own heavy industry, attracting more investment, which was accompanied by technological improvements on all fronts. By 1880, steel steamships eased ocean travel, initiating the massive wave of "new immigration" to the United States. Each industry fed on the others: steel machines mined and transported coal and iron, which were used to produce steel, which was used to make machines, and on, and on.

By the early 1900s, a third stage of industrialization had emerged, its hallmarks being electrical devices and vehicles with internal combustion engines fueled by petroleum, including automobiles and airplanes. Whereas before, technical innovations had been the work of practical mechanics, now important innovations were increasingly based on research in pure science, especially in chemistry and electronics. The factory system, with its specialization of tasks and large hierarchical organization of formal roles, which had begun with textiles and grown with the heavy industries, now permeated the workplace. This dominance was evident not only in manufacturing but in merchandising and finance, emerging as the now familiar corporate office, housed appropriately in the steel structured skyscraper that marked the central industrialized cities of the twentieth century.

The Revolution in Ideas

The Industrial Transformation involved more than new technologies and organization of manufacture, for it was also a period of drastic change in political and social arrangements, and in the ways people thought about themselves and their world. With the rapid adoption of the printing press in the fifteenth century, partly the cause and partly the result of increased literacy, new ideas spread faster and farther than ever before. Accounts of the voyages of discovery circulated widely, challenging the world picture of Christian Europe.

The Bible is not much concerned with geography or astronomy, but these were topics of great interest to the Greeks and Romans, whose writings were "discovered" by Christian scholars (from Arab sources) in the twelfth to fourteenth centuries. Impressed by the common sense rationality of classical thought and convinced that its logical reasoning must lead to the same true conclusions as the revealed word of God, these churchmen set out to reconcile one with the other. In the process, they allied Christian doctrine with Greco-Roman geography and astronomy, especially as codified by the Roman scientist Ptolemy (ca. 90–168 AD). Two of Ptolemy's most important claims were that day and night are caused by the rotation of the sun around a stationary Earth and that the continents surrounding the Mediterranean cover most of the Earth's surface.

This latter notion was falsified by the time of Magellan's circumnavigation, for it was then clear that there was a New World and that the globe was mostly covered by ocean. If Ptolemy's geography was wrong, why not his astronomy? Soon—in 1543—Copernicus published his suggestion that a rotating Earth moved around the sun. Astronomers had long known that night and day could be explained by a rapidly rotating Earth as well as by a sun that circled the Earth, but a rotating Earth seemed absurd because it would cause persistently strong east winds, and objects would fly out from the surface by centrifugal force. It is not clear whether Copernicus really believed that the Earth moved or was simply demonstrating its mathematical plausibility, but Johannes Kepler (1571–1630) and Galileo Galilei (1564–1642) certainly believed it, and along with Isaac Newton (1642–1727) and a few others they used the idea to launch modern science.

Galileo was a forceful proponent of the heliocentric theory, using his telescopic observations of Earth's moon's rugged mountains and of Jupiter's four largest moons to chip away at the classical notions that heavenly bodies were unblemished and invariably rotated around the Earth. In his famous controversy with the Church, Galileo was forced to publicly recant his heresy, but there is no doubt that he continued to believe it. In the long run, Galileo's celestial discoveries were less important than those he made about earthly objects, especially his law of the pendulum: the period of a pendulum (i.e., the time it takes to swing back and forth) does not depend on the weight of its bob nor on the amplitude of its swing but is proportional to the square root of its length. For Galileo, this had no relevance to his celestial discoveries because, like the Greeks and Romans, he believed that the planets operated on completely different principles than those that governed objects on earth.

Kepler, a contemporary of Galileo, was a strange mix of modern astronomer and classical astrologer (Koestler, 1960). Like the ancients, he believed that the planets moved through the heavens on crystalline spheres, and he spent much of his career trying to deduce the musical notes that these spheres sounded as they rotated on their axes. His other major goal was to prove mathematically why there were only six planets. (Today, we know of eight, after dismissing Pluto from the set.) Along the way, Kepler discovered three precise mathematical laws that describe the motion of planets, the most famous being that orbits are elliptical, not circular as nearly everyone had believed for 2,000 years.

With the discoveries of Kepler's celestial laws and Galileo's terrestrial laws, the stage was set for Newton's great synthesis. His *Principia*, published in 1687, showed that all of them could be derived from four simpler universal laws that apparently governed all mechanical motion, whether in the heavens or on Earth. The same gravity that keeps planets and comets in elliptical orbits around the sun accounts for the regular motion of the pendulum or the fall of an apple, and all of these motions can be described in precise mathematical detail! Newton's was an awesome, perhaps unsurpassed, intellectual achievement that became an inspiration and a model for other scientists, who produced an array of precisely confirmed theories in mechanics, electromagnetism, chemistry, optics, and thermodynamics. Progress in the physical sciences has continued unabated, forming the basis for modern high-technology industry.

Precise mathematical theories did not come so easily in geology or biology, but these were nonetheless carried along by the scientific ethos. Darwin's theory of evolution (1859), which described the gradual emergence of advanced species (presumably including humans) from lower forms of life, and the discovery that the Earth's age was far older than 10,000 years, flatly contradicted the account of creation in the Bible. This new knowledge caused some intellectuals to distance themselves from traditional beliefs, but science was not really a serious challenge to religion because most people ignored, dismissed, or were oblivious to the contradictions. Even today, in the face of irrefutable evidence that the Genesis story of creation is incorrect, many religious fundamentalists, far more in the United States than in Europe, regard it as literally true.

While the religion of preindustrial Europe held up well enough against science, it had a harder time in competition with rival religions. During the sixteenth century, antagonistic sects rose up against the Catholic Church on many fronts across northern Europe. Collectively known as the "Protestant Reformation," these protests destroyed the monolithic sway that the Catholic Church had held over most of Europe throughout the Middle Ages.

The Catholic Church has weathered severe storms including the fall of Rome, the split of the Eastern Orthodox Church in Constantinople from the Roman Church in the eleventh century, the simultaneous reign of two and then three popes, all antagonistic to one another (1378–1417), and several periods of corruption. Therefore, it is unlikely that dissatisfaction over church abuses, about which Martin Luther railed, was the primary reason for the success of the Reformation. Certainly, it was a factor. The Renaissance popes, enjoying the wealth and secular pleasures of commercial Italy, were extreme in their "venality, amorality, avarice, and spectacularly calamitous power politics" (Tuchman, 1984: 52). But the Reformation had deeper causes, which were essentially the same as those leading to industrialization: rising commerce and the political consolidation of nation states.

The medieval Church had dominated Europe when the continent was divided into numerous small political units, and in practical politics, popes often succeeded in challenging kings. The Church justified its own privileges and those of the aristocracy, assuaging the poor peasantry with a doctrine of otherworldliness, preaching that life was a temporary state to be suffered until one's final rewards were received in the Kingdom of Heaven. As commercial activity brought increasing affluence, people of the Renaissance opted to enjoy this world rather than waiting for heaven. Wealthy merchants of common birth had no interest in sustaining the privilege of a hereditary aristocracy and its clerical allies, preferring instead the new Protestant sects that opposed the traditional power structure, disposed of the Church hierarchy, and saw virtue in commercial activity. At the same time, monarchs who had become sufficiently powerful to challenge the Church often saw good reason to do so. Henry VIII, once a devout Catholic, disposed of the Catholic Church in England because the pope would not grant him a divorce; in the process, he benefited by confiscating Church property and taking control of English religious life. Most Protestant sects took on a nationalistic character, an expression of opposition to the continental overlordship of the traditional Church. Even those countries that remained Catholic reformed their churches along nationalistic lines, as in France where the Gallican Church subordinated the interests of the pope to those of the monarch.

The middle class, growing in both size and affluence, expressed its opposition to the aristocracy in politics as well as in religion. Why should the nobility enjoy special privileges simply by virtue of birth, especially when many commoners had accomplished more and were richer? Didn't common citizens have the right to control their own lives and to choose their own government by popular vote? By the nineteenth century, this doctrine of equality and liberty, called "Liberalism," advocated a constitutional government of democratically elected parliaments, with guaranteed freedoms of religion, speech, and press. (The liberal and conservative positions in contemporary American politics are both consistent with nineteenth-century Liberalism.) Obviously, it was an ideology of self-interest, the upwardly mobile commoner against the aristocrat, but there were truly altruistic elements as well, for by the nineteenth century, Europeans—if not Americans—abolished slavery.

Liberalism was an important justification for the American Revolution (1775–1783), the French Revolution (1789–1792), and the independence movements in Latin America (1808–1825). The drastically different outcomes in these cases were due largely to their differing class alignments. In the American case, there was no resident aristocracy to block the aspirations of common citizens. The issue was simply to eliminate foreign (British) taxation and control over local affairs, which was accomplished fairly easily. This done, the Americans who held power before the Revolution were essentially the same people who held it afterward. In contrast, France did have a privileged aristocracy that naturally resisted the French revolutionaries, producing a bloody seesawing between Liberal and royalist forces, which lasted for decades.

Much of Europe was involved throughout the nineteenth century in a similar struggle, complex in class terms but including as one component the aristocracy attempting to preserve its traditional privilege against the new interest groups produced by industrialization. In the case of Latin America, most of its countries won their independence from Spain or Portugal, but lacking sizable middle classes they could not sustain their new democracies, and most lapsed into dictatorships from which they have only recently emerged.

Liberalism did not completely champion equality and liberty. While advocating democratically elected governments, it often regarded the proper voters to be men who owned property. Liberalism was, after all, an ideology for those who were benefiting most from industrialization, not for the growing masses of wage laborers and urban poor. As Karl Marx pointed out, factory owners had different interests than factory workers, and these classes would naturally pursue their own ends. While the comfortable middle class advocated its rights against aristocratic privilege, the hard-pressed working class—Marx's proletariat—pushed its own cause through labor unions and socialist movements. Joined by skilled artisans and craftsmen, whose occupations were threatened by mechanization, and by sympathetic intellectuals, these groups argued for better working conditions, voting rights for everyone, and a general shift of wealth and power from the "haves" to the "have-nots." Growing rapidly in number, the workers pressed their demands—sometimes peacefully, sometimes not—with more success in Western Europe and America than in Eastern Europe. By the time of World War I, most of the industrialized nations had passed laws to prohibit the worst exploitation of workers, and most men (but not women) had the right to vote. Britain and France were parliamentary democracies, but much of Europe still had powerful monarchs, including Russia, Germany, and Austria-Hungary.

World War I

World War I did not end Europe's Industrial Transformation, which continues today, but it does mark the end of that period since 1500 when Europe rose to, and then held, a dominant position over the rest of the globe by virtue of its industrial power.

The causes of World War I are complex, but one important factor was the existence of several powerful nations in Europe by the end of the nineteenth century, each trying to expand its trade markets, military power, and territorial control, often at the expense of the others (Keegan, 1999). The political consolidation of powerful monarchies had begun centuries earlier with the rise of Spain, France, and Britain, among others. Italy was finally unified (1859–1890) and, more importantly, Otto von Bismarck achieved the union of the German states (1864–1871). Overseas, the United States expanded its territory all the way to the Pacific Ocean.

The most powerful of these nations were the most industrialized ones: Britain, France, Germany, and the United States. Other nations of Europe—and, oddly, Japan—sought to emulate them. Everyone recognized the importance of colonial possessions for industrialization, for colonies are sources of raw material, markets for finished goods, and places to invest accumulating capital. With merchant and naval fleets of steel steamships, with the newly constructed Suez Canal (1869) allowing Europeans direct access to the Indian Ocean, and with railroads crossing territories heretofore accessible only with great difficulty, the industrial powers extended their presence to most other areas of the world.

Some nonindustrialized countries welcomed this presence, some had little to say about it, and some actively resisted. The Chinese wanted nothing of "barbarian" goods or culture from

Europe, but they would trade their silks, tea, and porcelain for opium, which the British brought from India. When Chinese authorities tried to stop the drug trade, Britain's gunboats fought two Opium Wars (1839–1842, 1857–1860) to enforce its trading rights. The Japanese, too, wanted to bar Western trade; this time, American gunboats under Commodore Perry opened the way (1853–1854). While much of this European and American imperialism was generally profitable, some was not, especially the mad scramble for possessions in Africa. In the period 1885–1900, the European powers, motivated largely by their own rivalries, staked out nearly the whole continent for themselves, leaving the Africans no say at all.

By the beginning of the twentieth century, the world had become a stage with powerful industrialized actors playing the leading roles, each trying to upstage the others. European diplomats were primarily concerned with managing constantly shifting coalitions, for adversaries one day might be allies the next. There were a few stable alignments, especially the unalterable opposition between France and Germany, the result of France's humiliating loss of the territory of Alsace-Lorraine in the Franco-Prussian War (1870–1871). Britain was also opposed to Germany, largely because Germany insisted on building a powerful navy that Britain regarded as a threat to its essential control of the seas. On the other side, Germany had a long-standing alliance with neighboring Austria-Hungary. But many other alignments among Europe's major powers were in flux.

In the years before the war, two opposing coalitions had solidified. On one side were Germany, Austria-Hungary, and Italy. On the other were Britain and France, traditional enemies, now joined with Russia to oppose the German bloc. Some observers of the time thought these powerful coalitions would balance one another, thus preventing a war from occurring. But if war did come then the interlocking treaties could draw all the nations in together. That is what happened.

With the wisdom of hindsight, we know that the leaders of Europe were wholly ignorant of what they were getting into. Surely this, too, was a major cause of the war, for it is hard to believe that they would have been as incautious as they were if they had a clear idea of the consequences. Realize that the heads of state knew one another—many of the monarchs were related, and some of them saw the politics of nations as nearly equivalent to playing out personal rivalries and jealousies. Furthermore, it was generally understood that an occasional limited war was an extension of diplomacy, an instrument of policy to be used when other inducements failed.

The event in 1914 that precipitated the war is not too important since probably any number of events could have set off a similar chain reaction. As it happened, Archduke Francis Ferdinand, heir to the throne of Austria-Hungary, and his wife were assassinated by a Serbian nationalist. (Serbia was a small country on the southern border of Austria-Hungary that had broken away from the long-decaying Ottoman Turkish Empire.) As punishment, Austria-Hungary gave Serbia an ultimatum, threatening invasion if it were not met (July 23), so Serbia mobilized to repulse the attack (July 25), and in response, Austria-Hungary formally declared war (July 28).

Russia, seeing in the conflict a chance at its long-sought goal of moving closer to the Mediterranean Sea, mobilized to support Serbia against Austria-Hungary (July 29–30). In the meantime, Germany warned Russia that it must stop the mobilization or Germany would enter on the side of its ally Austria-Hungary. At the same time, Germany demanded from France (Russia's ally) a declaration of neutrality. Since Germany did not receive satisfactory responses, it declared war on Russia (August 1) and France (August 3), so they declared war back. The German army quickly moved to attack France, invading Belgium to get there (August 2–3), which led Britain to honor its treaties of support in case of attack.

Thus, within two weeks, the major nations of Europe were joined in war, formally because they were honoring mutual defense treaties, but actually because each saw the war as a way to gain some immediate goal against a rival. The French could retrieve Alsace-Lorraine from the Germans, Germany could enhance its stature on the continent, Britain could checkmate the German naval buildup, and Russia could move toward the Mediterranean. For Italy, which was supposed to side with Germany and Austria-Hungary, it was finally more opportune to join the other side. However, Italy's defection was made up for by Turkey, which joined Germany and Austria-Hungary because it saw the opportunity to make gains against Russia. Even Japan entered the war—on the side of France, Britain, and Russia—to occupy German possessions in the Pacific.

The carnage was unprecedented. About 10 million people were killed in the four years of fighting (1914–1918), an average of over 6,000 per day! An indirect cause of this high toll was the rapid increase in population during the nineteenth century, which had accompanied industrialization. At the same time, nations were changing from professional to conscript armies, and these two factors combined to increase the number of men in the field. A more direct cause of the terrible casualty rate was the application of industrial technology to warfare. Railroads and steamships transported these large armies and their supplies to the war zone. The internal combustion engine powered trucks that moved men and material from ports and railheads to the front, or from one front to another, and it powered submarines that struck at Atlantic shipping. Airplanes and armored tanks were used for the first time in wartime, but another twenty years would pass before the full effectiveness of this combination would be demonstrated in the Nazi blitzkrieg tactics. The machine gun gave World War I its special character, for together with rapid-fire field artillery, it provided the defense a strong advantage over offensive forces. Dug into their trenches, a few defenders with machine guns firing ten rounds per second could hold off a much larger number of attacking troops. As a result, defensive positions became nearly impregnable and the war bogged down, especially on the Western Front, where the lines moved less than ten miles over the first three years of fighting.

In Russia, the enormous cost in lives and money, added to preexisting problems, produced the Communist Revolution of 1917, the abdication of the tsar, and Russia's withdrawal from the fighting. However, this loss was offset by the entry of the United States, which had finally declared war against Germany, its fresh troops helping to break the stalemate. The war ended in 1918. The monarchies of Germany, Austria-Hungary, and Turkey were dissolved, and their empires were broken up. Austria-Hungary ceased to exist as an entity.

The centuries-long period of strong monarchs was over for Europe's major powers; their governments were now parliamentary democracies of one form or another. Most of these countries, the victors as well as the vanquished, lost a generation of men and were under enormous financial debt as a result of financing the war and paying for its damages. The United States was the only big winner, physically undamaged and with relatively few casualties (116,516 dead, 204,002 wounded). Its industrial and military might expanded to the fullest, creditor to most of Europe, America emerged from World War I the richest and most powerful nation on earth.

4

Twentieth-Century Superpowers: The United States and the Soviet Union

> There are . . . two great nations in the world tending toward the same end . . . the Russians and the Americans. . . . Their starting point is different, and their courses are not the same: yet each of them seems marked out by the will of Heaven to sway the destinies of half the globe.
>
> —Alexis de Tocqueville, 1835

While Western Europe was the power center of the world, Russia and America were growing on the periphery, their potential strengths clearly apparent by the nineteenth century. With no important barriers to territorial expansion, incorporating vast natural resources and rapidly growing populations, and freed by distance from the costly struggles of the central powers, these two giants came by different roads to dominate global politics in the last half of the twentieth century. Their nuclear arsenals held each other—and the rest of the globe—under a threat of annihilation that dissipated only when the Soviet Union foundered. This was a dark period of hostile but (luckily) not massively lethal standoff between the two behemoths. It is bracketed by the two great turning points of the twentieth century, beginning with World War II (1939–1945) and ending with the collapse of the Soviet empire (1989–1991).

World War II resulted in the deaths of perhaps 50 million people (compared to 10 million in World War I), leaving Europe and Japan devastated, while America was virtually untouched. As in World War I, the United States, safe behind its ocean moats, could mobilize enormous resources for the war effort, creating an industrial and military capability—now including nuclear bombs—that far surpassed those of any other nation. When the war ended in 1945, with much of foreign industry destroyed, American manufacturing production was half of the world's total (Bairoch, 1982). In the postwar years, America funded the restoration of many of the industrialized nations— including its former enemies, Germany, Japan, and Italy—partly from altruistic impulse but also for fear that the weakened economies of Europe would be ripe pickings for the Soviet Union.

The wartime alliance between America and the Soviets broke apart as soon as the war ended. Despite the Soviet Union's appalling losses (20–25 million dead), it retained the largest intact army in Europe; and with Germany defeated, Soviet-American animosity escalated, especially as the USSR imposed its control over other countries of Eastern Europe, forming an empire of "satellite" nations. When the Soviets tested an atomic bomb in 1949, the option of a new war became too costly. Instead, the two superpowers entered a "Cold War" of competition in economic and political spheres, in the arms race and the space race, and by supporting opposing sides in local wars throughout the Third World.

During the Cold War, Americans (and Soviets) came to interpret politics in terms of a bipolar world, divided between hostile American and Soviet camps with few actors who were not on one side or the other. We saw world communism as a monolithic conspiracy attacking the Western Democracies, and American involvements in Korea and Vietnam were justified largely in those terms. This image was seriously undermined in the late 1960s when it became clear that a split had occurred between the Soviet Union and Maoist China, bringing them to the brink of war. With more than a fifth of the world's population, China now stood as a wholly independent communist entity, one which President Richard Nixon could eventually approach in friendship. By the 1980s, when the United States had better relations with both China and the Soviet Union than those two countries had with each other, the picture of a bipolar world divided into solid communist and capitalist blocs had become obviously inadequate.

Furthermore, differing industrial growth rates had greatly altered the concentrations of economic power from what they had been in the postwar years. By the 1980s, the Soviet economy, after first expanding, had become stagnant. The United States, despite a recession, was still vigorous, but it no longer dominated the global economy as it had in the 1950s because other nations were reviving. Japan's tremendous postwar expansion produced an economy that eventually surpassed that of the Soviet Union. The nations of Western Europe, increasingly intertwining their economic affairs, reemerged as world players. Still, the United States and the Soviet Union remained the two most powerful nations on earth in combined economic and military terms, and they remained ideological and political adversaries until the last decade of the twentieth century.

Background of the Soviet Union

The Union of Soviet Socialist Republics (USSR) comprised fifteen republics, of which Russia (including Siberia) was by far the largest. Since the USSR's collapse, these are now fifteen separate nations. Altogether, the USSR was larger in land area than Canada and China combined, covering most of the "top half" of Eurasia and, like the United States, containing about 5 percent of the world's population. Most of the Soviet land was farther north than in the United States and had a less hospitable climate, with average annual temperature below freezing in 60 percent of the country. Having much land that was unsuited to agriculture, the Soviet Union, and Russia before it, had always had problems growing enough food (Kerblay, 1983).

By virtue of its size, the Soviet Union's aggregate economy was second only to that of the United States for most of the period after World War II. However, in the years before its demise, Soviet income per capita was below that of Western Europe or Japan, and its material lifestyle was low compared to industrial nations of the West. In military power, including nuclear weaponry, the Soviet Union was roughly equal to the United States.

Most (70 percent) of the Soviet population was concentrated in the western quarter of the country, which is sometimes regarded as part of Europe. The best agricultural land is here as well as the major cities of Moscow, Leningrad (now St. Petersburg), and Kiev. Most of these westerners are Slavs—Europeans who speak Russian or other Slavic languages and come from a religious tradition of Eastern Orthodox Christianity. Slavs constituted the bulk of the nation's leadership in government, the military, the arts and sciences, and the Communist Party. In contrast, a third of the Soviet population was Asian in culture and language and Muslim in religion. These people, concentrated in central Asia, were poorer, more rural, and less educated than the Slavs and were on the periphery of the Soviet industrial society.

Russian history has always reflected this contrast between Europe and Asia. In the thirteenth century, Mongols led by the grandson of Genghis Kahn conquered eastern Russia and occupied Kiev (now the capital of Ukraine). The defending Slavs thought that strong rulers were essential against the Mongolian threat, and over the next centuries a succession of tsars centered at Moscow expanded the Russian empire in the east against the Mongols and in the west against neighboring European powers. The tsars were autocrats like other European monarchs at that time. But while the West was then experiencing a growth of commerce and general revitalization from the "Dark Ages," Russia was too far distant from these activities to be affected. While medieval feudalism was breaking down in Western Europe, its peasantry increasingly freed from bondage to their lords, Russia's serfs remained closely tied like slaves to the landlords. In industrialization, Russia lagged 100 years or more behind, as if striking a compromise between Europe and Asia.

It is instructive to compare the United States and Russia as they were in the mid-nineteenth century, shortly before they entered the Civil War and the Crimean War, respectively. The most obvious similarity was that both had grown to enormous size, each reaching the distant (but opposite) shores of the Pacific Ocean. Both had very large and rapidly growing populations; Russia held about one quarter of Europe's people by 1850, while the United States, with less than half that, had become larger than any of the other European powers. Both of these giants were viewed from the capitals of Western Europe as cultural backwaters, not only because they lacked social niceties but also because both nations kept portions of their own people enslaved. About 15 percent of Americans were black slaves, while perhaps half of all Russians were bonded serfs.

Despite slavery, the United States was an intensely liberal democracy, dedicated to individual freedom of thought and action. That these freedoms were limited to whites and men meant that America was backwardly racist and, like Europe, sexist. While these seem contradictory positions today, they were not always seen that way in the nineteenth century when many Americans could defend the institutions of democracy and slavery in the same breath. Russia, in contrast, had little taste for liberal democracy. Its tsars remained the most autocratic of the European monarchs, suppressing all of the democratic reforms that were eventually adopted by the Western Europeans.

The American Civil War was fought partly to resolve the place of slavery in a democracy but also because the North and South had sharply different economic interests. A factory system had grown rapidly in the northern states, while the South retained its plantation economy. The United States was industrializing more quickly than any other nation, while Russia was lagging. In 1860, America's share of world manufacturing output was still well behind that of Great Britain, but it had already overtaken Russia and would soon pass France. While America had only 40 percent of Russia's population in 1860, its urban population was more than twice as large, it produced more than twice as much iron as Russia, its energy consumption from modern fuel sources was fifteen times as large, and it had more than thirty times more railroad track. On the other hand, America's army on the eve of the Civil War comprised only 26,000 men compared with Russia's mammoth force of 862,000. The disparity between the economic power and the military power of these titans was perhaps never greater than at this point (Kennedy, 1987).

Within a few years of one another, America mobilized two armies to fight its Civil War (1861–1865), and the massive Russian army lost the Crimean War (1854–1856) to the allied forces of Britain, France, and Turkey. The outcomes of these conflicts illuminate the strengths and weaknesses of the two rising giants. The North won the Civil War because its greater industry and population could support an army until the South eventually ran out of men, money, and material needed to carry on. By the war's end, America had the most powerful and technologically advanced army in the world, although it was soon demobilized, considered as needless. The Crimean War, in contrast, showed the large Russian army technologically deficient as a military power. Although Russia had a fair-sized navy, the Allies had more steam-driven ships that were better armed. Russian soldiers were equipped with muskets while Allied troops had rifles with five times the range. The Russians had no railroad south of Moscow to transport troops and supplies, nor was there enough factory capacity to keep the army stocked. These failings and the loss of the war were a shock to Russian self-esteem, spurring attempts to modernize the society along the Western industrialized model, including the abolition of serfdom. It is ironic that "advanced" America and "laggardly" Russia formally freed their enslaved peoples at virtually the same time.

For most serfs, emancipation only replaced formal bondage with a system of financial obligation that gave them little more freedom than they had before. The nobility and gentry—1 percent of the population—still owned nearly all of the agricultural land and continued to do so up until the Russian Revolution in 1917, and the peasants still lacked a decent living standard. Some of the peasantry moved to the cities to join the growing factory workforce, although industrialization progressed slowly compared to Western Europe and Japan, both of which made rapid strides in adopting the new technologies. When the tsar went to war against Japan over problems in Asia (1904–1905), modern Japanese military forces scored an impressive win over the still backward Russians. This unpopular war, added to deteriorating domestic conditions, stimulated a series of strikes and demonstrations against the tsar, which are loosely called the "Revolution of 1905," but tsarist forces soon reasserted autocratic control with its censorship, secret police, and political imprisonment.

At the outbreak of World War I in 1914, Russia allied with Britain and France against Germany and Austria-Hungary. By the end of 1916, the Russian army, no more efficient than it had been in the Crimean and Russo-Japanese Wars, had nearly 6 million dead, wounded, seriously ill, or captured, with no end in sight. The privations of war made already poor conditions in the cities and countryside far worse. Life was dismal and was deteriorating.

It did not help that Tsar Nicholas II consistently resisted any serious reform movement as a threat to royal control. Never regarded as a very competent ruler, Nicholas's stature suffered further because of his unpopular German wife, Alexandra, and her irrational tie to the fraudulent holy man, Rasputin. Believing that Rasputin could stem their hemophiliac son's bleeding, the tsar and tsarina accepted his advice even on matters of state until the monk was murdered by a group of aristocrats in 1916. By that time, many of Nicholas's subjects were blaming him for the debacle of the war.

In early 1917, worker riots broke out in St. Petersburg (later renamed Leningrad and now St. Petersburg once again) to protest food shortages. Troops sent to suppress the rioters joined them instead. Seeing little chance to regain control, Nicholas abdicated in March, bringing the Russian monarchy to an end. What quickly emerged as a replacement government was a coalition of workers and soldiers, liberals and socialists. Their immediate goals were to relieve shortages of food and other supplies, to set up a democratically elected government, and to reinvigorate the war against Germany.

One faction of revolutionaries, the Bolsheviks led by Vladimir Lenin, argued instead for an end to the costly war so that all energies could be devoted to building a new socialist society along the lines envisioned by Karl Marx. As the Russian army continued to falter, Lenin's proposal for a withdrawal gained support. Lenin also wanted to transfer land rights from the aristocracy to the peasantry, obviously a popular proposal in the countryside. By November, the Bolsheviks had become dominant in St. Petersburg and Moscow, and Lenin dissolved the newly elected Constituent Assembly, ending Russia's brief experiment with liberal democracy.

The Marxist-Leninist-Stalinist State

Lenin quickly made peace with Germany so he could concentrate on consolidating his position and fulfilling his revolutionary program. The Bolsheviks, renamed the Communists, nationalized the land, banks, and industry; confiscated church property; established government-controlled labor unions; and distributed land to the peasantry. An overriding goal was to create the Marxist ideal of a classless society, where everyone would share equally the material fruits of production. Naturally, the propertied classes who stood to lose by this arrangement vehemently opposed it.

These truly revolutionary changes, imposed on top of the existing disorder, created immense problems of administration. Lenin resorted to censorship and police action, suppressed his opposition, and ruled as undemocratically as the tsars before him had. By these means, Lenin was able to hold control against conservative forces inside Russia as well as more moderate socialists who objected to his repressive methods. Lenin's colleague, Leon Trotsky, organized the Red Army, which by 1921 successfully defended the regime against remnants of the tsar's army as well as European, Japanese, and American forces, all trying to dislodge the new government. With these successes, the communists in 1922 reorganized the areas under their control as the USSR.

The "Marxist-Leninist" nation that emerged was different in important ways from the communist society envisioned by Karl Marx. Widely regarded today as a brilliant historian, Marx was one of the European "socialists" who maintained that workers should share fully in the fruits of their labor rather than having profits accumulate in the hands of a small privileged class. Marx had observed the evils of industrialism as it existed in Europe in the mid-1800s, where factory owners often increased their riches by exploiting the poor workers of city slums. He saw in this an intrinsic conflict of interest between the propertied "capitalist" class, which financed the factories, and the powerless "proletariat," who had only their own labor to sell. Marx believed that the plight of the workers would eventually become so intolerable that they must rise up against the capitalists in violent revolution. This seemed to Marx the inevitable destiny of every capitalist industrial society. Indeed, Marx observed the rebellions that swept Europe in 1848, seemingly confirming his analysis. Marx sided with the downtrodden workers, urging them to hasten the revolution that he felt was inevitable. He optimistically thought that once the workers had seized the factories and thrown the capitalists from power, they would share these resources with everyone, creating a classless society where each person contributed what he could and took only what he needed. In this utopian vision of a cooperative commune-like—or communist—society, there would be no need for government, which would eventually wither away, leaving the people free, amply provided for, and happy.

Lenin had to reshape Marxism to fit the Russian situation. In the first place, Russia was still primarily an agricultural society, slow to industrialize, and so the exploited class was not urban factory workers so much as rural peasants—hence Lenin's emphasis on farmland redistribution. More importantly, government did not wither away in the Soviet Union or even take on liberal democratic forms but instead became one of the most totalitarian regimes of the twentieth century. The justification was that an uneducated peasantry was incapable of establishing the new socialist society, encircled by hostile governments; and it must be guided by a small cadre of intellectual militants: the Communist Party. Total control of Soviet society by the party and its police organ (called the KGB after 1954), with political terror an important tool, is not a Marxist idea. Rather, Lenin saw the benefits of transferring these traditional features of tsarist despotism to his new communist government, and most people accepted them because they had never known anything better. If Marxism had been applied to a nation with an established liberal democratic tradition, the outcome would likely have been different.

With so much of the Russian population an uneducated peasantry, there were relatively few people capable of running government besides those who were already doing so for the tsar. As a result, Lenin had little choice but to keep on many of the bureaucrats and military officers who held similar positions before the revolution (Pipes, 1984). This was a compelling reason to strengthen the Communist Party into an overseer group of loyalists who could monitor the essential activities of those whose loyalties were in doubt. The party became the primary ruling instrument of the Soviet Union, its members directing and watching over most of the nation's institutional activity. At its top was the Politburo (pronounced "polit-bureau") of ten to sixteen full members who set basic policy for the nation. The general secretary of the Communist Party, who led the Politburo, was for all practical purposes the nation's political leader. The party elevated and dismissed members from within, without relying on public elections.

After Lenin's death in 1924, his successor, Joseph Stalin, reshaped the Communist Party and its operations. Stalin's goal was to spur agriculture and industry, the outputs of which had fallen since the Revolution. He hoped to accomplish this by planning the entire Soviet economy as if it were a single corporation, specifying the kinds and numbers of products to be produced. Once these targets were set, planners could work backward to determine needs for raw materials and workers and for the kinds of factories and machinery that should be built. Stalin expected to gain efficiency with this kind of coordinated central planning, which differs from the fragmented capitalist "market" economies where numerous firms and individuals make their own decisions to purchase or manufacture various products. The Soviet government, overseen by the Communist Party, became the administrative apparatus that formulated these central plans and monitored performance. All of the country's factories, farms, stores, schools, and theaters were thus administered through bureaucratic hierarchies headed in Moscow

(Hough and Fainsod, 1979). As the economy grew, these administrative offices expanded into an enormous bureaucracy with its own inefficiencies.

Stalin was highly successful in accelerating heavy industry but not agriculture, which had special problems. His plans called for eliminating small privately owned farms and combining them into larger state collectives that could be farmed more efficiently. The more prosperous among the peasants—the *kulaks*—resisted surrendering their property; they slaughtered their animals and held back on their planting. As a result, Stalin eliminated the kulaks as a class. Millions were killed or sent to labor camps. These agricultural disruptions led to catastrophic famine in 1933, claiming millions more lives (Johnson, 1983).

Stalin's terror soon turned inward on the Communist Party and the Red Army. In the "Great Purge" of 1936–1938, the dictator searched out anyone who might be disloyal. The army's senior officer corps was decimated, with roughly 60 percent of its 684 highest ranked commanders arrested (Hough and Fainsod, 1979). At the Communist Party's congress of 1939, only 37 survivors were present from among the 1,827 delegates who had attended the prior congress in 1934. In the period 1934–1939, 4 or 5 million party members and officials were arrested on political grounds, and 400,000 to 500,000 were executed without trial (Kerblay, 1983; Johnson, 1983).

Ronald Reagan, as president of the United States, called the Soviet Union an "evil empire." Whether or not one agreed with Reagan at that time, it seems a fair characterization of Stalin's regime, which rivaled Hitler's in savagery. After Stalin's death, his "crimes" were denounced by his successor, Nikita Khrushchev, and subsequent Soviet leaders distanced themselves from these affairs.

World War II

Relations between Stalin and Hitler were in character. In August 1939, the month before Hitler started World War II by invading Poland, he and Stalin signed an agreement not to fight one another, this despite Hitler's well-known hatred for communism. The Nazi dictator did this to escape the dilemma that Germany had faced during World War I of having to fight on two fronts—Russia to the east and the other Allies to the west. Why did Stalin accommodate his natural enemy? The nonaggression pact was the result of a secret deal between the two leaders, with Hitler agreeing to let Stalin take over eastern Poland and the Baltic nations of Lithuania, Latvia, and Estonia, while Stalin let Hitler have western Poland. In 1941, Hitler ditched the agreement and invaded the Soviet Union, causing Stalin finally to join the Allies.

World War II is often called the "good war," its participants the "greatest generation," meaning that for most of the Allies (excepting Stalin), there was a clear moral correctness in opposing Nazi attempts at conquest and genocide. Today, most Germans agree that Hitler was an evil man. This virtual unanimity about which side was ultimately right and which was wrong can hardly be found for any other war and surely not for World War I, Vietnam, or the U.S. invasion of Iraq.

Unlike Stalin, Hitler and his Nazi Party were elected to govern. Germany had been humiliated by the Treaty of Versailles, which ended World War I. Stripped of its military power and burdened by huge reparations payments, Germany entered the depression years of the early 1930s in dismal shape. Hitler preached a revitalization of German pride and strength, blaming most of the nation's ills on the Jews and communists. Named chancellor in 1933, after the Nazis won a plurality of seats in the Reichstag, he quickly suppressed basic civil liberties including freedom of press and the right to assemble, outlawed all political parties but the Nazis, and made himself dictator. Germany's experiment in democracy after World War I had not worked well, its many political parties always squabbling, so the nation was not very sorry to see it end. With his power established, Hitler began to fulfill his promises of economic revival—largely by building up the military—and by controlling the Jews and communists. At the end of the decade, Hitler had widespread support among the German people (Shirer, 1960).

While Hitler prepared for war, the Japanese were following the same path. As the only industrial nation wholly in Asia, Japan sought to establish a large sphere of economic domination across its side of the Pacific. Toward this end, its armies invaded China in the 1930s, but the more potent counterweight to Japanese ambition was America. Hitler also saw the United States as a potential impediment to his expansionist aims; while America had not joined the fighting at the war's outbreak in 1939, it was an active supplier of the Allies, and American sympathies were clear. So Germany and Japan (and Italy) agreed in 1940 to support one another against American interference. The Japanese opted for a preemptive strike to immobilize the American threat, and on December 7, 1941—a date President Franklin Roosevelt claimed "will live in infamy"—its airplanes surprised and largely destroyed the American naval fleet stationed at Pearl Harbor in Hawaii. In hindsight, this was one of the ultimate errors of the war, ranking with Hitler's invasion of the Soviet Union, for by bringing in the mammoth power of the United States, Japan ensured its own defeat and that of Germany.

The impact of World War II can hardly be overstated. It was one of the pivotal and certainly the most costly event of the twentieth century. The war severely damaged or temporarily destroyed most of the industrialized nations and many less developed areas of the world. More than 20 million people were killed in the Soviet Union, 8 million Germans, 4 million Poles, perhaps 35 million in all of Europe, including 6 million Jews, Gypsies, and homosexuals who were exterminated by the Nazis as if they were vermin. Twelve million were killed in China; over a million Japanese died, one-tenth of them by the two nuclear detonations at Hiroshima and Nagasaki. Altogether, nearly 50 million people—2 percent of the population of the world—were killed in World War II.

At the war's end in 1945, the United States and USSR were in wholly different positions. The United States had 405,000 troops dead and 670,000 wounded, but these casualties were light compared to those of other major participants. America's home territory was unscathed, its industrial and military strength had never been higher, and it held a monopoly on nuclear weapons. The Soviet Union, with one-third of its men killed, was in ruins, although its army was intact. Despite the United States' superiority, it and the other Western allies withdrew from most of the foreign territories they had captured, although they left armies of occupation in Germany and Japan. Stalin, in contrast, kept control over lands entered by the Red Army, including Poland, the Baltic nations, Hungary, Romania, and Bulgaria; and although he had few troops in Czechoslovakia, he was able to impose his authority there too. President Harry Truman, fearing that other wartorn nations might fall to the Soviets—Greece, Turkey, and Iran were especially vulnerable—sponsored the highly successful Marshall Plan, which used American money to finance economic recovery in Europe and bolster those nations most vulnerable to Soviet takeover.

The situation was more complicated in Germany where there was continuous friction between the Soviets, who occupied the eastern portion of the country, and the Americans, British, and French, who held the western part. This division became a seemingly permanent separation between two new nations: West Germany (aligned with the Western allies) and East Germany (part of the Soviet bloc). Thus, Hitler's nation was fractured in two, to the relief of those who feared that a united Germany might rise once more to threaten Europe.

By the early 1950s, there was ample reason to believe that most of the world was divided into hostile communist and capitalist blocs, each bent on destroying the other. The United States, Canada, and their European allies (now including West Germany) had formed the North Atlantic Treaty Organization (NATO) military alliance as a counter to communist expansion. In response, a few years later, the Soviet Union and its satellite nations coordinated their armies under the Warsaw Pact. In Asia, Mao Zedong's forces won the long Chinese civil war, shifting the most populous nation on earth from the American camp to the communist bloc. Communist insurgent movements were active elsewhere in Asia. On the Korean peninsula, the communist armies of North Korea and China were fighting the capitalist forces of South Korea and the United States. Despite the

"Happy Days" mind-set of American culture during the 1950s, it was not a good time for international relations.

After Stalin

After Stalin's death in 1953, Nikita Khrushchev emerged from among the Politburo membership as his replacement (Taubman, 2003). A loyal associate of the dictator, Khrushchev stunned his own nation and the West by denouncing Stalin's crimes of political terror. That the Party accepted Khrushchev's accusations and instituted legal reforms as a protection against arbitrary personal rule such as Stalin had exercised indicates how dreadful the Stalinist regime had been even to those who were a part of it.

It was timely for Stalin to be replaced by a more moderate leader, for in the same year that he died, the USSR exploded its first hydrogen bomb and shortly afterward developed missiles that could carry these warheads to the United States. The stakes were becoming too high to risk heating up the Cold War, and Khrushchev claimed that the communist and capitalist powers could coexist. Soviets and Americans avoided direct confrontations for fear of triggering a more damaging war than either wanted. Instead, they postured and fought "by proxy," backing opposing sides in numerous local wars that broke out among the less developed countries that were then gaining their independence from the weakened European powers. Only once—the Cuban missile crisis of 1962—did the two powers come head to head.

President John Kennedy had approved the covert "Bay of Pigs" invasion of Cuba, aimed at overthrowing Fidel Castro's communist government. To Kennedy's embarrassment, the invasion was a fiasco, easily repulsed by Castro. Khrushchev claimed in his memoirs that the Soviets then placed nuclear missiles in Cuba to discourage the Americans from a repeat invasion of the island, although another motive may have been to counter American nuclear weapons aimed at the USSR. In any case, American spy planes spotted these missiles being installed barely 100 miles from Florida.

For years, American nuclear missiles had been stationed next to the Soviet Union in Turkey. Ironically, Kennedy had earlier ordered them removed, but his order was never carried out, so there was a symmetrical situation, each side having nuclear arms near the other's border. Kennedy might have offered an even exchange, the Turkish missiles for the Cuban missiles, but he thought this would show weakness. He also rejected direct air strikes against the missile sites as too risky. Instead, he publicly announced the presence of the missiles, demanding that the Soviets remove them. They denied that any missiles were there.

Kennedy ordered a naval blockade to intercept Soviet ships carrying arms to Cuba, at the same time placing American nuclear forces on maximum alert. With Soviet cargo ships steaming toward the blockade line, it was unclear if they would attempt to breach it; and if so, should the American navy fire on them? Then Khrushchev sent Kennedy a letter offering to remove the missiles if the president would pledge not to attack Cuba. Before Kennedy could respond, Khrushchev sent a second letter, this one offering to remove the Cuban missiles if Kennedy would dismantle the Turkish missiles. In the meantime, an American spy plane was shot down over Cuba, heightening the tension. Kennedy ignored the second letter, writing to Khrushchev that there would be no American invasion of Cuba if the missiles were removed. Also, through his brother Bobby, the president secretly assured Khrushchev that the American missiles would be removed from Turkey. Khrushchev agreed to this arrangement, ending the crisis. Shortly afterward, the Soviet missiles were removed from Cuba. Later, the American missiles were removed from Turkey (Fursenko and Naftali, 1997; Mazur, 2005).

There has been much debate about how close the superpowers actually came to war. Some argue in retrospect that the nuclear forces of the United States were in 1962 so far superior to those of the USSR and the logistical problems so great if the Soviets were to fight in the American hemisphere, that Khrushchev had no option other than to back down. Perhaps, but Kennedy and his advisors certainly believed they were on the brink of war. Dean Rusk, then secretary of state, later revealed that the president, as a fallback position, had secretly arranged for the United Nations secretary general, acting as a neutral mediator, to propose an exchange of Cuban for Turkish missiles, to which Kennedy would agree. This contingency never arose, and so Kennedy emerged the clear winner in American eyes. Others argue that Khrushchev and especially Castro were the real winners for receiving American guarantees that there would be no repeat invasion of Cuba.

Stung by the Cuban episode, the Soviet Union bolstered its nuclear armaments; and the United States responded in kind. Yet despite their enormous and growing weapons stockpiles, the two superpowers evolved a reasonably stable relationship after the Cuban missile crisis. They remained ideological adversaries, jockeying to outdo one another on the world scene but never again approached the brink of war. The Soviets provided supplies to America's Vietnamese enemies but never interfered directly in that war. When Soviet troops invaded Afghanistan, the United States supplied weapons to the Muslim opposition (among them, Osama bin Laden); but America's direct actions against the Soviets were nonaggressive: halting grain sales and boycotting that year's Olympic Games in Moscow.

Evil Empire or Pragmatic Rival?

Was the Soviet Union of the 1980s still an "evil empire," as President Reagan claimed at the time? Or had it reformed sufficiently since Stalin's death that it might have been more properly regarded by the U.S. as a pragmatic rival, operating in its own self-interest pretty much as any other nation would operate?

In 1985, when the Politburo selected Mikhail Gorbachev to lead the Soviet Union, the country was still a police state, severely limiting the freedom of its own people and of those in its satellite nations. Newspapers and television could not carry information or opinions then disapproved by the Communist Party nor could these be published privately. Interpretations of history, politics, and artistic expression could not contradict the party line. There were restrictions on religious practice; people of certain religions, including Jews, were targets of special discrimination. Citizens who violated or protested these restrictions could be harassed by the police, placed under surveillance, lose their jobs, or be arrested and imprisoned or confined in psychiatric hospitals. Citizens did not have the right of free assembly, and no political party other than the Communist Party was permitted. Citizens voted in elections where there was only one candidate for each office. The Soviet people were not free to emigrate or to travel outside the country without special permission, nor could they live in restricted locations such as Moscow unless they had a permit. Still, this was an improvement since Stalinist times.

Accompanying the increasing tolerance for dissent that began in Khrushchev's regime, there arose in the USSR a visible dissident movement to protest the lack of freedoms and the continued arms race between the Soviet Union and America. This movement gained strength after the Arab-Israeli war of 1967 (the "Six Day War"), which intensified Jewish self-identity among many Soviet Jews who had previously ignored their religion. Confronting the USSR's anti-Israel foreign policy and the persistent Russian tradition of anti-Semitism, many of these Jews requested permission to emigrate to Israel or America, but most were denied it, often losing their jobs and sometimes facing trial and prison in the process. Year-by-year changes in the way Soviet authorities treated these dissidents—how many were allowed to emigrate and who was sent to prison or into exile—became a closely watched indicator of the state of human rights in the Soviet Union.

But most Soviet citizens, even before the Gorbachev era, were not rebellious dissidents and apparently did not approve of the dissident movement. Most residents of the USSR appreciated their country, admired its leaders—past as well as present—and were loyal and patriotic citizens. A survey of nearly 3,000 Soviet émigrés who moved to the United States in the period 1979–1982, most to be united with families or ethnic and religious communities, showed that even those who left the USSR were fairly positive about it; 66 percent had been satisfied with their housing, 64 percent with their job, and 59 percent with their overall standard of living, although more than 75 percent were dissatisfied with the availability of consumer goods in their homeland (Milnar, 1987).

From a Rashomon perspective, it is not surprising that Soviet citizens—even those who emigrated—appraised their homeland in positive terms. Just as Americans generally approve of our own society and see our own actions as morally correct, so too did the Soviets, and so do citizens of other nations.

American journalist David Shipler makes the same point in describing a discussion about foreign policy that he once held with a group of Moscow teenagers, avid members of a communist youth group:

> I said (to them) I thought both superpowers were playing a dangerous game by selling arms and competing for influence in the third world, magnifying local conflicts and doing nobody, least of all the local people, any good. The reaction to this was shocked and indignant, utter disbelief that I was equating the United States and the Soviet Union. The United States was doing these things, several youngsters asserted, but not we Russians. A boy . . . lashed out: "The United States is an imperialist power that sucks the blood from smaller, weaker countries, taking their harvests and giving them nothing. The Soviet Union, by contrast, does what it does to help these countries. . . ."
> My simple effort to maintain that neither of our countries always acted out of the noblest of motives ignited an astonishment and rage that swept the entire room, twisting the youngsters' faces into hurt and anger. Unwittingly I had challenged a most fundamental vision of a world divided neatly into good and bad, and the teenagers . . . were each struggling, fighting to regain that vision and keep it intact. It reminded me of the view from my teenage years in the 1950's, when the world was cut unambiguously by an iron curtain, and America still stood on the side of purity. Here was the mirror image of that naive and comfortable time, staring back at me in complete incomprehension. (Shipler, 1983: 127–28)

When he wrote this passage, neither Shipler nor other experts on foreign affairs expected the Soviet Empire to self-destruct within a decade. The disintegration of the Soviet system during the years 1989 to 1991 seemed to come out of the blue and was without precedent. One of the world's most powerful nations had never before collapsed so suddenly and completely without being forced to by an outside agent. This incredible conclusion ended the threat of nuclear Armageddon and left the United States as the world's sole remaining superpower. It is the only event in twentieth-century history that can be fairly compared to World War II in global importance.

Collapse of the Soviet Empire

Why did it happen? The most commonly heard—though surely oversimplified—explanation is that the Soviet economy was so inefficient that it collapsed of its own weight. Indeed, there were obvious signs of economic failure. Journalist Richard Reeves noted of Moscow in 1988, "The city is crumbling and cracked, grimy, rusting, leaking, peeling and flaking."

Reeves told of an "average" Soviet family, the Bayevs, profiled in a Moscow newspaper. The husband was in charge of loom maintenance at a silk mill and the wife was a laboratory technician, so they had two incomes. The Bayevs lived twenty miles from Moscow with their two children in a two-room apartment, 30 feet by 10 feet in size. They had a twenty-five-year-old refrigerator, a small black-and-white television, four bicycles (no car), four sets of skis, and a tape recorder (Taubman, 2003).

To compare the availability of consumer products in the United States and the USSR, Radio Free Europe calculated in 1987 how much work time it took the average industrial worker in Washington and Moscow to purchase sixteen common goods and services. The Muscovite had to work ten to twenty times longer than the Washingtonian to buy a chicken, a grapefruit, or a pair of jeans; and he had to work three to seven times longer to buy a liter of milk or wine, tea, a car wash, soap, a pair of men's shoes, or a washing machine or to hire a babysitter. Their work times were roughly equal for a cabbage or a postage stamp, and the Washingtonian had to work about twice as long as the Muscovite for a loaf of bread, bus fare, or a haircut (Taubman, 2003).

Despite problems with the Soviet economy and the economies of other communist countries, it seems implausible that this fully accounts for their collapse. After World War I, the Soviet-planned economy (harshly administered) had rapidly converted the USSR from an agrarian to an industrial society. During the 1930s, it escaped the Great Depression, a dire time for America and Western Europe, and it performed well during the recovery after World War II. When communist planners made their yearly allocation of resources, they always favored basic needs, the military, and heavy industry over unnecessary consumer goods, so the material lifestyle of communist society was never as luxurious as in the West.

During the 1970s, the American capitalist economy was staggering under the combined load of high unemployment, high interest rates, and high inflation. But as the U.S. economy improved during the 1980s, the Soviet economy did not, and their differences became starker. Citizens of the Soviet Union and its satellites were well aware of their relative deprivation, which was vividly apparent across the Berlin Wall, which separated the communist sector of that city from free and affluent West Berlin. For communists further from the border, images of wealthy and luxurious lifestyles could be seen in American soap operas, beamed across the Iron Curtain by the Voice of America.

Another overly simple theory is that President Ronald Reagan's hard line toward the Soviet Union, backed by his military buildup and especially his proposed "Star Wars" missile defense system (see chapter 5), pushed the USSR over the edge. No doubt the arms race was a costly drain on both powers, especially the USSR, with its smaller economic base. But even if the Reagan doctrine forced the Soviets into a subordinate military position, it did not cause their entire society to fall apart.

To get a wider view of the collapse, it is worth scanning additional problems that contributed to that end. The year 1979 is a convenient one with which to begin an account of the USSR's worsening external affairs. That was when the Soviets invaded Afghanistan, on their southern border, intending to return to power a pro-Soviet government. Like the Vietnam War for the

United States, the Afghan War was a quagmire for the Soviets—
a no-win hellhole that became intensely unpopular at home. The
prior year, the Vatican selected a new pope, John Paul II. His significance lies in the anomaly that he was Polish, not the usual
Italian, and was intensely nationalistic. In 1980, when workers at
a Polish shipyard began an illegal strike for better conditions,
they unwittingly ignited a political protest movement that went
much further because the pope, and later the newly elected
American president, Ronald Reagan, used their respective pul-
pits to rally support. The strikers' organization, called "Solidarity," was outlawed in 1982, but the tumult continued. When the
pope eventually visited the Polish city of Lubin in 1987, a million
people attended the mass over which he presided, not so much
from religious fervor as to support the Solidarity movement, its
goal now broadened to ending Poland's communist regime.

In the meantime, inside the Soviet Union there were certainly
economic problems, worsened by a collapse in oil prices during
the 1980s. (The USSR was a major oil exporter.) Soviet citizens became increasingly envious of the material comforts and civil liberties they envisioned in the West. The Soviet dissident
movement, begun in the Khrushchev era, faulted the Soviet leadership for its authoritarianism and its buildup of nuclear armaments. The men in the Politburo, mostly holdovers from Stalin's
generation, were old and stultified. Their leader since 1964,
Leonid Brezhnev, became decrepit in office and died in 1982. He
was succeeded by another old man, former KGB chief Yuri Andropov, who died in 1984. Andropov was replaced by another
elder, Konstantin Chernenko, who died the following year.

Thus, in 1985, the Soviet position was dismal overall. It was
mired in Afghanistan. Poland was restive, and discontent was
spreading to other satellite nations. The economy was stagnant,
dissidents were complaining, and leaders were dying in rapid
succession. Less tangible but equally important, many Soviet citizens suffered a malaise, a depressing feeling that their lives, and
their society, were going nowhere. Under these conditions, the
Politburo finally selected as general secretary a younger, more
vigorous man—someone who could move the empire forward
again. This was Mikhail Gorbachev, a loyal communist and pro-

tégé of Andropov, who had risen quickly through the party apparatus. Almost certainly, the Politburo gave Gorbachev a mandate to reform the system, to break out of the doldrums into which the nation had fallen.

Gorbachev accepted the diagnosis of Soviet ills as the result of excessive military spending, inefficient central planning of production, the inattention of workers to their jobs because of a lack of personal rewards, and widespread censorship within the society (Gorbachev, 1987). He initiated a program of political and economic reform whose main themes were *glasnost* (freedom of expression) and *perestroika* (economic liberalization), which together promised a drastic redirection of Soviet society toward the political and economic forms of the industrial democracies. At first, many Western observers regarded Gorbachev's words as empty rhetoric, but then deeds followed as censorship was loosened and political dissidents were freed. In a series of summit meetings, Gorbachev developed a surprising rapport with President Reagan, a staunch anticommunist.

In 1988, the Soviet Union, under Gorbachev, liberalized its political structure, shifting power from the Communist Party to a truly democratically elected parliament, which in turn elected a president to lead the nation. Gorbachev became the first person elected to the newly empowered presidency.

One of the most dramatic of all these changes was the USSR's loosening hold on its satellite nations, which from time to time had attempted to break free of Soviet control. Yugoslavia had succeeded, establishing itself as an independent communist nation shortly after World War II. However, when Hungary tried to withdraw from the Warsaw Pact in 1956, Soviet troops invaded the country to suppress its rebellion. In 1961, Khrushchev ordered the Berlin Wall built to block East Germans from escaping the Soviet sector of that city. In 1968, Soviet troops entered Czechoslovakia to squelch its attempt at independence.

The stunning events of 1989 revealed a full reversal of policy. The Soviet Union allowed—even encouraged—liberal reforms in its satellite countries. First Poland, then Hungary and Czechoslovakia, moved toward full democracy, including legal political parties in opposition to the Communists. East Germany opened its borders, allowing its citizens to cross the Berlin Wall freely. This dramatically marked the end of communism in East Germany, and very quickly the two German states, East and West, began plans for reunification. By 1990, noncommunist governments were in power in most of the satellite nations. Indeed, it was no longer clear that they were still satellite nations.

Gorbachev accepted—even presided over—these reforms, but he certainly did not intend to destroy the Soviet system. Events took on a momentum difficult to control. By 1990, the Baltic republics of the USSR—Lithuania, Latvia, and Estonia—which had been forcibly incorporated by the Soviets on the eve of World War II, protested that they, too, wanted to be free of Moscow's control. This, finally, was going too far for Gorbachev. He sent troops to quell the protest, with loss of life. But neither he nor many other Soviets could stomach such Stalin-era repression, and soon he allowed the Baltic republics to depart.

Back in Moscow, some in the Old Guard were apoplectic as they watched their system fall apart. In the summer of 1991, they attempted a coup, placing Gorbachev under house arrest. But the coup, ineptly carried out, quickly failed, and Gorbachev was freed. Despite his restoration to office, it was clear to everyone that the game was over. With varying degrees of enthusiasm, all of the republics opted to go their own way as independent nations. By mutual agreement, at the end of 1991 the Soviet Union ceased to exist (Dobbs, 1997).

Future Superpowers?

The twenty-first century began with the United States as the world's sole superpower—no doubt a temporary status. At this time, there are four obvious candidates to match or even overtake America, perhaps within a few decades.

A New "Soviet Union"

Russia (including Siberia), by far the largest remnant of the Soviet Union, continues to hold huge assets that Alexis de Tocqueville recognized in the nineteenth century. To those, we must add a citizenry that is well educated and technically skilled, big deposits of petroleum and natural gas, and a large arsenal of nuclear weapons.

Following the Soviet collapse, Russia, under the unsteady leadership of Boris Yeltsin, continued to plummet. Its economy and morale were in far worse shambles after the breakup than before. And now it was torn by rebellious Chechens, wanting their own independence. After Yeltsin, former KGB agent Vladimir Putin became president, leading a stabilization and apparent upturn. Russia ended 2003 with its fifth straight year of economic growth, its gross domestic product (GDP), a convenient measure of economic activity, increasing nearly 7 percent annually since 1998. (U.S. GDP averaged about 2 percent growth between 2000 and 2003.) Because Russia's manufacturing sector remains dilapidated, its abundant supplies of oil, natural gas, metals, and timber account for more than 80 percent of exports, leaving the country vulnerable to swings in world prices (CIA, 2004). Recently, oil prices have been high, allowing Russia to finance improvements.

While maintaining good relations with the West, President Putin's actions hint at a centralization of power under his administration. Russia and eleven of the former fifteen republics are now joined into a loose Commonwealth of Independent States to cooperate on trade and other matters. (The former Baltic republics—Lithuania, Latvia, and Estonia—wanted no part in it.) Still, like Humpty-Dumpty, it is unlikely that the old USSR can be made whole again. It is plausible that Russia may reunite with some former republics, perhaps Belarus or Ukraine. That does not imply—but it does not preclude—a return to Russian-American hostilities with their juxtaposition of huge nuclear arsenals.

The European Union

No other European power, not even Germany, is very likely to dominate all of the others. It is their joining together as the European Union (EU), encompassing by 2007 twenty-seven nations with 450 million inhabitants, that has produced a megaeconomy, roughly equal in size to the economy of the United States.

This integration began shortly after World War II with the implausible partnership of formerly bitter enemies, France and West Germany, also joined by Italy, Belgium, the Netherlands, and Luxembourg. In 1951, the six nations formed the European Coal and Steel Community, pooling their coal and steel markets to improve trading efficiency. Another important goal was to bind West Germany and France into mutual dependency, to blunt the possibility of another European war (Hitchcock, 2003). The members removed all customs duties in 1968. The economic success of these lowered trade barriers was quickly apparent.

Seeing the advantages of economic cooperation, other European nations sought membership in what eventually became the European Economic Community (later renamed the European Community by the Maastricht Treaty in 1992). The United Kingdom, Ireland, and Denmark joined in 1979; Greece in 1981; Spain and Portugal in 1986; Austria, Finland, and Sweden in 1995. As membership grew, areas of cooperation expanded. The Treaty of Maastricht formalized the community as the European Union, granting joint legislative powers to its European Parliament and Council of Ministers. Within the EU, people, goods, services, and capital move freely across national borders, much as they travel from state to state in the United States. In 2002, twelve EU members began using a common currency, the euro.

In 2004, the EU took a momentous step toward European unification, adding ten more nations, including the Czech Republic, Slovakia, Poland, and Hungary—all former Soviet satellites—and three former Soviet republics, Lithuania, Latvia, and Estonia. In doing so, the EU essentially buried the Cold War fracture of Europe into free and communist worlds. Two more former satellites, Romania and Bulgaria, joined in 2007.

There are three major criteria that candidate nations must meet to enter the EU: (1) they must be stable democracies, extending civil rights even to minorities; (2) they must have a functioning market economy, able to cope with competitive pressures within the Union; and (3) they must adopt the entire body of EU law, which implies that they generally share the political and economic aims of the Union.

Turkey is moving slowly toward membership, attempting to satisfy these conditions by strengthening its democracy and improving its treatment of minority Kurds. Some in the EU object to adding a Middle Eastern Islamic nation to the European Christian community. There are fears that impoverished Turks will flood the European labor market, accepting low wages and diluting traditionally European cultures. On the other hand, a great benefit of admitting Turkey would be to diminish the centuries-old division between the Christian and Muslim sectors of Eurasia.

To date, the great successes of the EU lie in economics and peace. The partnership clearly improved the prosperity of postwar Europe and virtually eliminated the prospect of future wars between member nations. There have been lesser dividends too. Increasingly, the EU produces unified policies regarding environmental protection, the settlement of trade disputes, and the pursuit of international criminals and terrorists.

As a political federation, the EU is nothing like the United States of America, and it is unlikely to meld into a "United States of Europe." With different languages and cultures, Europe's nations are reluctant to cede their sovereignty or independence. Some, notably Britain, refused to convert their national currency to the euro (but may in the near future). Most have no desire to pursue a unified European policy toward the U.S. or toward the rest of the world. The Europeans utterly failed to stop the tragic disintegration of Yugoslavia during the 1990s, requiring American leadership (and warplanes) to halt the genocide of Bosnian Muslims by Serbs. Europeans have no wish to place all national armies under a unified European command. For these reasons, the EU will not soon emerge as a "national" superpower like the U.S. or the former USSR, but certainly it will be a major player on the global stage.

Japan

During the 1980s, Japan was widely regarded as an emerging superpower. Disarmed after World War II, it chose to remain

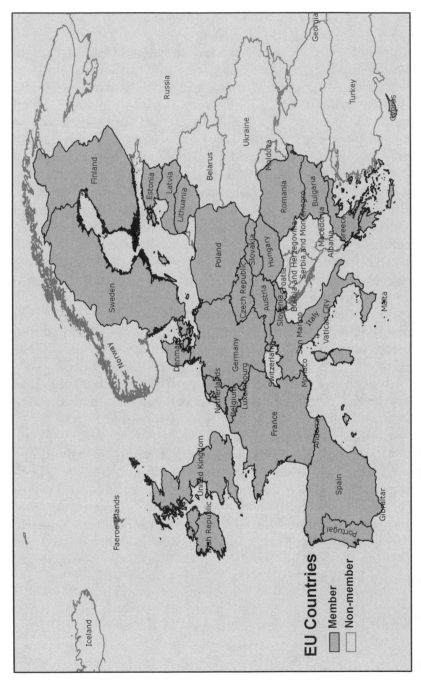

Figure 4.1. The European Union as of 2007

relatively demilitarized, keeping a military force about half as large as the largest armies in Western Europe. It was in economic rather than military terms that Japan excelled. With roughly twice the population and half the land area of France, Japan's industry expanded spectacularly in the decades after 1945. If the Japanese had maintained that growth rate, their gross domestic product would have soon surpassed that of the United States. The economy has since faded but could surge again.

As the first industrialized nation wholly in Asia, Japan was and remains an enigma to Westerners. On the one hand, its industry, technology, and commerce are similar to those in Europe and America. On the other hand, its oriental traditions and customs are mysterious to other developed nations. How did this country, so far in distance and culture from the European core of the Industrial Transformation, become modern so quickly and do it so well?

A unified Japanese empire existed by the fifth or sixth century AD, its civilization strongly influenced by Chinese culture and Buddhism. Agrarian Japan developed into a feudal system at about the same time as medieval Europe and functioned very much like it. Lordly families served by samurai warriors allowed peasants to use the land in return for their allegiance and a share of the crops that were grown. Japan's divine emperors remained in the background during this period as real power was held by hereditary military dictators called "shoguns." Eventually, a prosperous merchant class developed, again paralleling trends in Europe.

By the sixteenth century, Portuguese and Dutch seamen had established minor trading relations with the Japanese, and missionaries had introduced Christianity. But Japan saw little of value in Europe and limited these contacts. In 1853–1854, Commodore Matthew Perry's steam-powered gunboats coerced Japan to open its ports to the United States. The Japanese, impressed by American military might, decided that the best way to avoid domination was to achieve such power themselves. Over the next half century, with remarkable speed, Japan imported the industrial transformation from the West.

Commodore Perry's successful intrusion had discredited the shogun in the eyes of many Japanese. Opponents promoted the idea of bringing the emperor back to real political power, from the largely ceremonial position to which he had been relegated for centuries. While this sounds like a return to ancient tradition, in fact it was a way to legitimate the elimination of the shogunate, uniting those who wanted modernization with the traditional samurai who were obligated to honor the emperor. In 1867, the last shogun voluntarily resigned to the Emperor Meiji; hence the period is called the "Meiji Restoration." In reality, the "restoration" was an overthrow of the whole feudal system, including the lordly families and their samurai retainers, replacing it with a constitutional monarchy patterned on German government (Toriumi, 1973).

A new army, based on French and German models, with Western uniforms and modern armaments, used commoners as soldiers rather than samurai warriors. When some of the samurai eventually revolted against the Meiji changes, they were defeated by this new army, thus verifying the superiority of modern methods over traditional warfare. During the half century of Meiji reforms, the Japanese were guaranteed civil liberties, literacy was increased through compulsory education, and peasants were given legal ownership of their lands. Railroads, telegraph lines, steamships, central banking, postal systems, and industrial methods were copied from Europe and America. British and French textile processes were adapted to silk cloth making. Among the imports from America, baseball became a Japanese passion.

With its new military power, Japan also copied Western imperialism, beginning in the 1870s to forcibly "open" Korea and China, as Perry had opened Japan. A clash of expansionist interests with Russia led in 1904–1905 to the Russo-Japanese War and Japan's heady victory over a major European power. Joining the Allies in World War I, Japan took over Germany's colonial possessions in Asia and the Pacific, emerging as the dominant power in the East. In the hard depression years of the 1930s, Japan, like Germany, abandoned its democratic forms and adopted militaristic expansion as a national goal. The end result, of course, was the devastation of World War II.

As a condition of surrender in World War II, the Japanese were allowed to keep their emperor, although he was divested of political power, and he gave up claims to divinity. The American occupation forces, under General Douglas MacArthur, set up a fully democratic parliamentary system, including the revival of political parties and guarantee of civil rights. To some degree, these reforms were a return to those of the Meiji period, although they moved further in the liberal direction. Despite the venom that had marked Japanese-American hostilities during the war, the Japanese accepted American occupation with surprisingly little bitterness; and in fact, the culture took a strongly American slant. With a new constitution renouncing war, Japan accepted the United States' military protection in lieu of building up its own defense forces.

Japan's industrial rebirth began quickly, aided by the procurement booms caused by American involvement in the Korean conflict (1950–1953) and later the war in Vietnam (1961–1975). The chemical, steel, and shipbuilding industries grew especially fast and provided most of Japan's exports in the 1960s. Lacking fossil fuels and other natural resources, and with little agricultural land for the size of its population, Japan became the master trading nation, bringing in raw materials for its industries, transforming these into finished products, and then selling them both at home and abroad. Continuing its imitation of Western technologies, producing cameras, radios, cars, and computers, Japan's manufacturers first emphasized low cost but soon focused on quality, making products that were often better and cheaper than those manufactured in the West. Japanese expertise in many areas of high technology came to equal and then surpass that of the West. Tokyo and other cities were rebuilt as modern metropolises with skyscrapers, subways, and expressways. The lifestyle is now Western in many ways but is more "cramped" because there are so many people for the space.

Economic growth during the 1960s averaged a spectacular 10 percent yearly. This moderated to a still strong 5 percent in the 1970s, and 4 percent average in the 1980s. Growth slowed markedly in the 1990s, averaging less than 2 percent. Government efforts to revive economic growth have met with little success and were further hampered in 2000–2003 by the slowing of the U.S., European, and Asian economies (CIA, 2004). Still, Japan has one of the world's largest economies and may again shift into high gear.

China

In the fifteenth century, when Columbus "discovered" America, China had as good a claim as any to being the world's most advanced civilization. Its aristocracy took a peculiarly bureaucratic form, with entry into the mandarin class (civil service) dependent on scholarly examinations (implicitly favoring those of privileged birth). Its arts, crafts, and technology were unsurpassed in the medieval world, perhaps because China never suffered a period of cultural regression as prolonged as Europe's Dark Ages. Among the better known inventions that Europe borrowed from China are papermaking, printing, the compass, gunpowder, and cast iron. Eighty years before Columbus's voyages, Admiral Zeng He commanded Chinese fleets of sixty or more ships that crossed the Indian Ocean to visit the east coast of Africa. Zeng's own ship of nine masts was four times the length of Columbus's flagship, *Santa Maria*. If not for the Ming emperor forbidding more voyaging—his reasons are obscure— China might have discovered the sea route to Europe—with barely imaginable consequences.

By the nineteenth century, the industrial transformation of Europe and America had given them enormous advantages in wealth and power. It was not that China faltered but that the industrial nations surged ahead.

The collapse of China's more than 2,000 years of (occasionally interrupted) dynastic rule followed partly from the intrusion during the mid-nineteenth century of Western powers seeking trade with populous east Asia. Like the Japanese, the Chinese wanted none of the crudely manufactured Western goods, but the Chinese would trade their silks, teas, and porcelain for opium, which the British shipped in from India. When Chinese authorities tried to stop the trade, Britain's gunboats fought two Opium Wars (1839–1842, 1857–1860) to enforce its right to sell the drug. China ceded Hong Kong to Britain and granted unrestricted trading privileges in several of its cities.

While Japan industrialized, China did not. Its passivity might have been a sustainable posture if the Western presence had been limited to its protected enclaves. But American and European missionaries searched inland for souls and converted many of them. With trade and Christianity came steamboats and railroad track, telegraph lines and mining equipment, all offending nature's spirits and eliminating Chinese jobs. These modernizations—some envied, some hated—undermined the traditional system. By 1895, the newly empowered Japan wrested Korea from China, a humiliating defeat for the Chinese, who had long regarded the Japanese as an inferior people.

China's turn-of-the-century Boxer Rebellion was a nativist reaction against Western influences, a violent eruption of pent up anger and frustration over disintegrating traditions and worsening economic conditions (Preston, 2000). The Boxers were a loosely organized sect that attracted peasants from northern China. Adherents practiced ritualistic martial arts, evoking in foreign minds the image of boxers. They believed they could make themselves invulnerable to enemy weapons and summon up legions of spirit soldiers for allies. The Boxers hated missionaries and regarded converts as traitors, or "rice Christians," who sold their souls for food.

In the summer of 1900, Boxer mobs attacked isolated missions and railroad stations, killing and sometimes torturing in grisly manner perhaps 200 missionaries and engineers and tens of thousands of converts—hacking apart, skinning, burning to death, or burying alive some of their victims. In June, with approval from China's Empress Dowager, an elderly lady of remarkable power, deceit, and survivability, imperial troops helped the Boxers blockade hundreds of foreigners and thousands of Chinese Christians in the international port of Tianjin, eighty miles southeast of Beijing, and in Beijing itself. Eventually, an allied army of British, American, Japanese, German, and other contingents lifted the blockades. Afterward, Beijing was indiscriminately looted and brutalized by all nationalities. The old Empress Dowager had miscalculated in supporting the Boxers.

The victorious allies preserved the dynasty but imposed on her government a huge cash indemnity and required the execution of some of her pro-Boxer officials.

Shortly before her death in 1908, the Empress Dowager chose as the next occupant of the celestial throne a two-year-old boy named Pu Yi. He was the last emperor, deposed during the revolution of 1911. When the Japanese took control of Manchuria in 1931, they made Pu Yi head of a puppet government. He ended his life as a gardener in Communist China.

The 1911 revolution began almost accidentally as a military mutiny, with other parties quickly joining to overthrow the dynasty and its boy emperor. Dynastic rule was replaced by a republic, although at no time from 1912 until the Japanese occupation of 1938 did the government function well as a parliamentary system. The nation would for years be in continual turmoil. The major contenders became the American-supported Nationalist Chinese, led by Chiang Kai-shek, and the Soviet-supported Communist Chinese, led by Mao Zedong. During World War II, they briefly formed a united front against the Japanese but soon resumed fighting among themselves.

Mao's Communists won decisively in 1949 when Chiang and his followers fled the mainland for the large offshore island of Formosa. Renamed Taiwan, this island is today an effectively separate (and successfully industrialized) capitalist democracy, although mainland China continues to regard it part of greater China.

Under Mao's dictatorship, mainland China became highly regimented and propagandized. Although revered by his people for restoring order and destroying China's traditional elite, Mao did not greatly improve the material condition of most Chinese. His Great Leap Forward (1958–1961), which organized the peasants into communes and centralized agricultural planning, was intended to increase farm output. But the farmers, more knowledgeable than their government leaders about which crops to plant, had no say in these decisions, and they had no incentive to work hard because they were not rewarded for their labors. The Great Leap failed disastrously, causing famine and millions of deaths.

Losing influence because of this debacle, Mao attempted to regain control by encouraging the nation's youth to engage in the Great Proletarian Cultural Revolution (1966–1976), intended to purify the communist movement by rooting out revisionist thinkers. Intellectuals were especially victimized, and university education ceased.

Mao was the bloodiest dictator of the twentieth century, responsible for 70 million deaths in peacetime (Chang and Halliday, 2006). Accumulated dissatisfaction within the party over Mao's disastrous policies led to drastic revision after his death in 1976. Deng Xiaoping, himself a victim of the Cultural Revolution, was put in power and led a changeover from central planning to a market economy (Chow, 1987). First, he encouraged farmers in the communes to grow supplementary food on their own small plots, letting them keep the produce or sell the produce and keep the profit. This non-Marxist incentive system produced such rapid improvement in food production that profit making was allowed in other sectors. The result was a quadrupling of GDP between 1978 and 2003, the most sustained rate of high economic growth ever achieved by a large nation. Measured on a purchasing-power parity basis, China in 2003 stood as the second-largest economy in the world after the U.S. (CIA, 2004), although by other methods of comparison it ranks lower. Of course, the size of China's economy is largely due to its huge population. In per capita terms, the nation is still poor. Currently, China's economy continues to grow at about 9 percent yearly. There are now Chinese billionaires and sections of Chinese cities, especially Shanghai, Hong Kong, and Beijing, that look as modern as any Western city.

As this largest of nations—containing one-fifth of the world's people—continues to grow richer, it faces deepening problems. Roughly 100 million unemployed rural workers drift between villages or seek a livelihood in the cities. Class differentiation, anathema to Marx, is increasing. Economic development requires increased consumption of energy and materials, with heavy impacts on the environment. According to the United Nations, China has seven of the world's ten most air-polluted cities.

And despite freeing up its economy, China remains a political dictatorship.

China is like a powerful dragon moving in an uncertain direction. In Chinese culture, dragons are favored animals, bringing good fortune, so long as one avoids being burned in their fiery breath.

5

War

Warriors have been a favorite subject since the beginning of literature:

> In their midst was Achilles, arming himself in the armour that (the god) Hephaistos had made . . . First he clasped over his legs those fine greaves with their silver ankle-guards. Next he put the corselet about his chest and slung the silver-studded sword over his shoulders. Then he took up the great shield, which gleamed like another moon. . . . Then he lifted the strong helmet and set it upon his head, shining like a star and nodding its golden plumes. Achilles tried himself in the armour to see if it fitted and if his limbs had easy play—it seemed to lift him up in the air like wings.
>
> —Homer (Rouse, 1938: 235)

> The judges had now been two hours in the lists, awaiting in vain the appearance of a champion. . . . It was, however, the general belief that no one could or would appear (to defend) a Jewess accused of sorcery . . . At this instant a knight, urging his horse to speed, appeared on the plain advancing toward the lists. A hundred voices exclaimed, "A champion!—a champion!"

"I have come hither to sustain with lance and sword the just and lawful quarrel of this damsel. . . ."

"The stranger must first show," said Malvoism. "that he is a good knight and of honorable lineage. . . ."

"My name," said the knight, raising his helmet. "is better known, my lineage more pure, Malvoism, than thine own. I am Wilfred of Ivanhoe."

—Sir Walter Scott (1962: 454)

The Seventh Ulany Brigade held its annual officers' affair at the Europa Hotel . . . [which] brought out the cream of Warsaw. Gabriela . . . entered the ballroom on Martha's arm. Both of them saw him at the same time. In fact, every pair of eyes seemed set on the door as the epitome of a Polish cavalry officer, Lieutenant Andrei Androfski, entered. . . .

"Isn't he yummy," Martha said.

Gabriela was still staring.

—Leon Uris (1961: 33–34)

Why do men go to war?

First of all, it is an emotional high. The warrior is the most glorious and romantic male image, whether as tragic Greek demigod, chivalric knight, or dashing hussar. Is there a better way to spend one's youth than as a hero?

Preparation for war can be an exhilarating experience. Often, young men join up in a rush, urged on by young women and their elders, anticipating the grandest adventures of their lives. Not everyone wants to go to every war, otherwise there would be no need for conscription. The Vietnam War was so unpopular that some fled to Canada to avoid service. During the Civil War, wealthy young Northerners paid poorer men to take their places in the draft. Still, the eve of war can be an invigorating time, as in the opening days of World War I when soldiers on both sides became suddenly popular, treated with gifts of food and beer and kisses as they strolled the streets in their new uniforms, greeting friends and showing off to the ladies.

Even when bloodless preparation gives way to the reality of killing, some like famed test pilot Chuck Yeager find pleasure in the contest:

> I knew that dogfighting was what I was born to do. It's almost impossible to explain the feeling: it's as if you were one with that Mustang, an extension of that damn throttle. . . . With experience, you knew before a kill when you were going to score. Once you zeroed in, began to outmaneuver your opponent while closing in, you became a cat with a mouse. You set him up, and there was no way out: both of you knew he was *finished* . . . You picked your spot: slightly below, so you could pull up, lead him a little, and avoid being hit by metal when he disintegrated. When he blew up, it was a pleasing, beautiful sight. There was no joy in killing someone, but real satisfaction when you outflew a guy and destroyed his machine. That was the contest: human skill and machine performance . . . The excitement of those dogfights never diminished. For me, combat remains the ultimate flying experience. (Yeager and Janos, 1985: 66–67)

Another American warrior, President Theodore Roosevelt, expressed similar thoughts more poetically when he said, "Every man who has in him any real power of joy in battle knows that he feels it when the wolf begins to rise in his heart" (1926: 306).

Some others abhor fighting and take drastic steps to prevent it, but once the fighting begins they, too, usually join in. Group identity causes us to support "our" side against "them," an emotional response that occurs among nonhuman primates, too, and must have affected warfare throughout human existence on earth.

During the Agrarian/Urban Transformation, when the size of fighting forces grew to match the rise of states, newer incentives were added to these old motives for war. Quests for profit must have become increasingly important at that time and remain so today. National leaders can make important gains—territory, wealth, power, a place in history—from a successful war, but benefits accrue to others as well. Large armies need weapons, clothing, housing, transportation, food, and entertainment. Profits go to arms makers, farmers, merchants, and laborers, all of whom are contributing to the effort as factories and offices bustle with activity. In Germany and the United States, the Depression ended in large part because of jobs created by the buildup for World War II.

The Formal Command Pyramid

The growth of state armies must also have been accompanied by increased reliance on formal organization to control the fighting men, most of them personally unknown to one another or to their leaders. The command structure of a large army is pyramidal in shape, with one or a few leaders at the top and numerous followers at the bottom. Each intermediate rank has authority over the ones below and contains more men than the ones above. Subcommanders at each level stand atop their own pyramids but are, at the same time, part of a higher commander's larger pyramid. The authority invested in such large, formal command structures provided incentives for war that did not exist in the world of hunters and gatherers.

American culture stresses social equality and encourages us to request tasks from our subordinates rather than commanding them. As a result, we fail to appreciate the force of command, wondering why infantrymen would suicidally obey an order to leave their trenches and charge into barbed wire and heavy machine gun fire. The power of even a minor authority figure to enforce obedience is illustrated in the experiments of psychologist Stanley Milgram (1974). Here, a director, clad in a white lab coat, asks an adult subject to administer electric shocks to another person. In reality, the person receiving the shocks is the director's accomplice and is not actually being shocked, but the subject certainly thinks that he is. Following a script, the accomplice, who initially agreed to be shocked, now asks the subject to stop shocking him because he has a heart condition, which the shocks are aggravating. Typically, the subject agrees to stop. However, the white-coated director tells the subject that he *must* continue giving shocks to the unwilling recipient, insisting that the experiment requires that he go on even though the recipient of the shocks wants to quit. Remarkably, about half of all subjects follow the orders of the director, continuing to give shocks to the unwilling recipient!

The results of Milgram's experiment are startling. Subjects were ordinary American citizens. They were under no compulsion except the force of authority of the white-coated director. They could have refused to give any more shocks, as half of them did. But an equal number found the authority figure so compelling that they followed his orders completely, even at the risk of causing harm to the other person.

The power of authority bears much more strongly on a soldier who has a long-term relationship with his commander. One persistently gives orders that the other habitually obeys. Furthermore, the commander is backed by an aura of legitimacy and by the legal option of court-martial in case of disobedience, which carries the possibility of disgrace, imprisonment, or even execution.

At first glance, one might think that the supreme commander at the top of the pyramid is the most powerful authority for men at the bottom. In actuality, it is usually the subcommander in closest proximity to a man—the "local authority"—who is the most potent at giving orders. The importance of proximity in enforcing authority is demonstrated by another of Milgram's experiments in which the white-coated director is obeyed more often when he is in the same room with the subject than when he is in the next room, giving orders over the telephone. In a military organization, the officer who is nearby, who sees his men on a daily basis, who is close enough to communicate with them face to face, will have more power over them than a distant officer of higher rank.

Pressures on the soldier to obey come not only from above but from his peers too. Living closely together as a group, the collegial bonds of "buddies" or "comrades in arms" reinforce the norm of compliance to orders. Among both German and American soldiers in World War II, the major motive for engaging in combat was neither patriotism nor ideology but rather their reluctance to let down their buddies (Stouffer et al., 1949; Shils and Janowitz, 1948). A soldier is unlikely to disobey an order that is accepted by his friends.

All of these local forces converge on soldiers in the trench who are ordered to attack a machine gun emplacement. The sergeant who has led his squad through prior dangers now urges them to follow him as he begins the charge. Buddies on either side join in, yelling to bolster their spirits. Other units are advancing all along the line. A lieutenant with revolver in hand screams at laggards, threatening to court-martial or shoot anyone who stays behind. Hardly anyone does.

The concept of local authority—that nearby officers have more power over the men immediately under them than do higher-ranked but more distant superiors—explains the strange phenomenon of a coup d'etat, where the head of the pyramid is replaced against his will by agreement of those at the second level, and the rest of the organization accepts the replacement, continuing to follow orders as before. Today, successful coups occur most often in Third World monarchies and dictatorships where the government and military hierarchies are intertwined. Typically, a coalition of generals or colonels will plan the takeover as a surprise move, arresting the head of state and those of high rank who still support him. They designate a new head of state, usually one of their own number, and announce to the nation that a new government is in place. Unless the former head of state or his loyalists are able to repulse the plotters, the new hierarchy functions much as before only with new leadership.

There are times when the existing head of state is legally removed from office, perhaps by losing an election, and yet refuses to step down. As long as he can retain the support of the officers immediately under him, he may be able to retain his office and power, staging something like a coup d'etat in reverse.

These seem unlikely outcomes, for we would expect the people to rise up in protest and soldiers in the ranks to refuse orders from an illegal authority. Yet successful coups occur every year. When the military command structure is the major institution in the nation so there are no challenges from comparably powerful hierarchies based on religion, political bureaucracy, business, or the mass media, then all that the top military commander must do to take over or retain power is to make sure that he has the support of the officers at the level immediately below him. They,

in turn, have control of the next level down, for the local authority of these subcommanders is usually stronger than the distant
authority of the legal head of state, and so on down the line. The
chain of command remains intact, and those at the lower ranks
follow their orders as usual.

Since the head of state has his own local authority, it is exceedingly difficult for the officers at the second level to organize
their mutiny. Plotters who try to garner allies risk attempting to
recruit a loyalist who will reveal the plot. Therefore, they often
play their hand without having obtained consensus among the
second-rank commanders. Perhaps the chief of the air force has
joined the plot but the chief of the army refuses and escapes the
plotters. Each chief can order his branch to support his own side,
with the result that the nation's air force attacks its own army.
The aviators and soldiers, now shooting at each other, are simple
pawns in the game being played at the top of the pyramid.

The power of local authority also explains why soldiers
sometimes commit brutal acts that otherwise seem incompre-
hensible, as when a company of American infantrymen murdered more than four hundred defenseless civilians in the
Vietnamese village of My Lai (Walzer, 1977). Instructions of the
company's captain, who had stayed behind, were ambiguous according to later testimony, saying to leave nothing behind and to
take no prisoners, but also ordering only the killing of "enemies." Lieutenant William Calley, who led the unit into the village and commanded his men to kill nonresisting villagers,
including old men, women, and children, later claimed that he
was following the captain's orders. In any case, most of the men
obeyed Calley's orders, although some fired only after they had
been commanded to do so two or three times.

In attempting to justify this action, it has been pointed out
that Vietcong women and children often made murderous attacks against American soldiers, and it was impossible to know
who was a combatant and who a civilian. Yet some soldiers on
the scene clearly recognized the difference. A few of Calley's
men refused to fire their guns, some ran away, and one junior officer tried to stop the massacre by placing himself between the
Vietnamese and the Americans, but most did as they were told.

Ideals

So far, we have talked of incentives for war based on romance and competition, profit making, group identity, and the compulsion within formal command pyramids. Ideals also play a part, perhaps the major part, in justifying any war to its participants. We always have idealistic motives for inciting war or participating in it. The American Revolution was fought to break the bonds of political tyranny. The goals of the Civil War—depending on which side—were to preserve the Union and end slavery or to preserve the sovereign rights of the separate states. World War I made the world safe for democracy. World War II excised the Nazi cancer from Europe and avenged Japanese treachery. The wars in Korea and Vietnam were fought to halt the spread of communism. Opposing leaders of today's "War on Terrorism" offer moralistic rationales, as we saw in chapter 1.

Each side in every war invariably justifies its own participation with idealistic claims. This is the militarist version of the Rashomon effect. The rhetoric of warfare always appeals to high ideals and lofty principles in order to defend each side's position as right, valid, and honorable (Walzer, 1977).

Are these idealistic claims among the real reasons for war, or are they simply excuses that each side mouths to gain sympathy and support and to boost the morale of its troops? Did America really fight World War I in order to "make the world safe for democracy," as President Woodrow Wilson claimed? Probably not, considering that we entered the war on the same side as tsarist Russia, one of the least democratic nations of Europe. On the other hand, it does appear that Hitler fought World War II in part because he believed the Germans to be a superior people who were destined to rule over Europe (Toland, 1976), and that Americans fought in Korea and Vietnam partly because American presidents sincerely believed that communism's spread had to be stopped in these places before it engulfed more of the Free World. The best we can say here is that sometimes the stated ideals are real causes of conflict, and sometimes they are little more than self-serving rhetoric. It is easier to discern which is the case in hindsight than at the time the claims are made.

The Nuclear Weapons Problem

With so many incentives for war, ranging from emotional to material to idealistic, it is not surprising that nations fight so often. Set against all of the pro-war incentives, there are only two disincentives—death and destruction—and even these are not very weighty so long as they occur on the other side.

Industrial technology has enormously improved the efficiency of armies. Ten million were killed in World War I, 40 to 50 million in World War II. Nearly all of this slaughter was caused by conventional (nonnuclear) means, but it was the development of nuclear weaponry that made the potential for death and destruction so great that it must finally outweigh all the reasons why large wars have been worthwhile in the past.

When the first atomic bombs were constructed in 1945, they arrived too late for action against Germany, which was already out of the war, but were promptly dropped on Hiroshima, killing roughly 100,000, and three days later on Nagasaki, killing about 50,000. The morality of this action has been debated ever since, not only whether the bombs should have been used against people, but if so, should they have been dropped on cities, and was it necessary to drop a second bomb so quickly after the first? Defenders of the decision claim that it was preferable to an invasion of Japan, which would have cost a million lives. Critics claim that a demonstration blast would have been sufficient and that Japan was near to surrender anyway.

The decision must be understood within the context of its times. For four years, America fought a costly and bitter war against Japan, begun by the surprise attack on Pearl Harbor. Americans held blatantly racist notions about the Japanese, reinforced by atrocities committed against American prisoners such as those at Bataan. The tenacious resistance of Japanese soldiers in the battles for the Pacific islands, when they usually chose death rather than surrender, and the suicide attacks of kamikaze pilots, diving their explosive-laden airplanes into American ships toward the end of the war, fostered a belief that the Japanese would defend their homeland at all costs. Remember, too, that in World War II both sides had come to regard as acceptable tactics the devastating aerial bombardment of civilian populations. Massive Allied fire-bombings of Dresden, Hamburg, and Tokyo had each already killed about as many people as would die in Hiroshima or Nagasaki. In this context, the first atomic weapons were regarded like any other new weapon. They were made to be used.

The Eisenhower administration's postwar doctrine of "massive retaliation" threatened the Soviet Union with nuclear devastation in case of aggression against an American ally. General Douglas MacArthur, commander of American forces during much of the Korean War, considered using atomic bombs against China; but a few years later, reflecting a changing military and political mood, he urged that nuclear weapons never be used because they are too destructive (Manchester, 1978: 828). What had changed since Korea was not only the destructive power of nuclear weaponry but the loss of America's monopoly. After the Soviet Union's first test explosion of an atomic bomb in 1949 and a hydrogen bomb in 1953, it began producing long-range bombers so that by the mid-1950s the United States seemed vulnerable to a nuclear attack on its own soil. The image was emphasized during the Cuban missile crisis of 1962 when the superpowers came closer than ever to nuclear war. It became increasingly clear that this would be a no-win solution. Strategists came to the strange realization that the reason for making nuclear weapons was not to use them but to prevent their use.

The risk is not simply that a nuclear detonation will destroy a city. Hiroshima, Nagasaki, Dresden, Hamburg, and Tokyo—all ruined in World War II by nuclear or conventional bombing—are thriving again. Humanity is sufficiently resilient to absorb the destruction of a few cities and quickly rebuild as long as there is help available from outside the area of devastation. If damage from a nuclear war could be held to this level, such a war might not be much worse than World War II.

Several nations could start a nuclear war. Britain, France, China, India, and Pakistan acknowledge having nuclear bombs and delivery systems, although none of these forces compares to the American or Russian arsenals. Israel has not acknowledged its nuclear arsenal but surely has one. At this writing, North Korea and Iran seem close to having nuclear weapons, and probably additional nations are following this path. There is also the problem of contraband weapons, particularly those once belonging to the Soviet Union, reaching terrorist organizations. With so many players in the game, there is a good chance that a nuclear bomb will kill people within our lifetimes, whether by design or accident.

A full-scale nuclear exchange, as might have occurred between the United States and the Soviet Union, would have produced thousands of detonations across the land area of the two countries within a few days, severely affecting most of the Northern Hemisphere. Some experts forecast that the amount of soot and dust lifted into the atmosphere from fires would block out much sunlight, causing a prolonged "nuclear winter" with devastating consequences for earthly life; others claim that the human species would be wholly eliminated by a nuclear war, and still other experts doubt these most dire predictions. No one can really forecast the outcome of a nuclear conflict—first, because it might take many different forms, and second, because its effects would be unprecedented and too complex to model with certainty.

Arms control—international agreement to limit the number, kind, placement, and use of nuclear weapons—was the cooperative solution most actively pursued by the superpowers. Soviet-American arms accords had some success, halting nuclear tests in the atmosphere (by moving them underground) and thus eliminating radioactive fallout. By treaty agreement, no nuclear weapons are based in the Antarctic or implanted on the ocean floor outside of territorial boundaries, and none is continuously orbiting the Earth. The multination Treaty on the Nonproliferation of Nuclear Weapons commits signatories that do not have nuclear weapons to continue their abstinence; United Nations inspectors verify compliance.

Such treaties prohibit activities that the signatories are unlikely to do anyway. During the Cold War, treaties limiting the number and kind of weapons had little effect on the arms race because the agreed ceilings were high enough not to interfere with each side's armament plans. When treaty limitations do get in the way, they may be ignored, reinterpreted, or abandoned.

For example, the USSR built a radar facility at Krasnoyarsk that was quickly recognized by the West as a violation of the anti-ballistic missile (ABM) treaty, but the Soviets insisted for years—until they finally admitted the violation—that the radar was intended for nonmilitary uses that brought it outside the scope of the treaty. When the United States began serious work on the "Star Wars" missile-defense system, it reinterpreted the ABM treaty to allow this ostensibly forbidden activity. In 1986, President Reagan simply abandoned the Strategic Arms Limitation Treaty (SALT) II treaty—never ratified by the Senate but heretofore adhered to by both sides—when he chose to exceed its ceiling on the permissible number of nuclear weapons. Since the collapse of the USSR, cooperation between Russia and the United States has facilitated the deactivation of a large portion of the Soviet nuclear arsenal.

It is unlikely that the world will be rid of nuclear weapons in the foreseeable future. Even if these weapons were destroyed, the knowledge to make them would remain, and they could be relatively quickly brought back into production. When President Reagan and General Secretary Gorbachev briefly discussed full nuclear disarmament at their Reykjavik meeting in 1986, the disincentives against complete disarmament became salient. Although it was obvious to both sides that they did not need as many atomic warheads as they then possessed, it was equally clear that nuclear weapons did serve a useful purpose. In their absence, all of the usual incentives in favor of war reassert themselves.

The Strategy of Nuclear Deterrence

Think of two men, each holding a cocked revolver with a hair trigger to the head of the other. If one shoots then the other, in his death spasm, will also fire a killing shot. The analogy illustrates the situation of the United States and the Soviet Union during the Cold War, each aiming its nuclear arsenal at the other so that an attack by either would have triggered a situation of "mutually assured destruction" (MAD).

The basic assumption of nuclear deterrence is that no rationally acting nation will purposely set off a nuclear war, knowing that to do so would cause its own demise. This MAD strategy does not preclude a war starting through irrational action or by accident, but at least it seems to prevent outbreaks based on utilitarian calculation, such as those that initiated the two world wars of the twentieth century. Proponents of MAD point out that we did survive the Cold War, while skeptics believe that we courted disaster and were very lucky to survive.

Lacking real-life experience in nuclear warfare, military strategists depend upon hypothetical arguments about what might happen under one sort of threat or another. These issues of strategy, and associated questions about weapons policy, are rife with controversy, usually pitting "hawk" positions of political rightists against "dove" positions of the leftists.

Often, the arguments involve ways in which the MAD standoff may fail. Consider, for example, the possibility of breaking down deterrence by disarming an opponent, as if one of our two men, rather than shooting the other in the head, instead shot the revolver out of his hand. The disarmed victim would now be at the mercy of the attacker. This ability to disarm an opponent before he has a chance to retaliate is called "first-strike" capability, referring not just to shooting first but to doing it in a way that effectively blunts the opponent's capacity to shoot back.

The same situation would occur if one nation had the ability to destroy the other's nuclear weapons before they could be used. This became a real fear among American hawks in the 1970s, as Soviet missiles increased in number and accuracy, raising the specter of a surprise first strike, not against American cities but against missile sites and bomber bases, thus destroying our retaliatory capability. This done, the Soviets could dictate terms by threatening a second strike if we demurred, this time against our cities.

Dove strategists rejected this argument, pointing out that because radar-type devices do not work well under water, it would be virtually impossible for the Soviets to detect and destroy more than a few of our missile-carrying submarines. Since most submarines would have survived a Soviet first strike, our deterrent would have remained intact.

The hawks counterargued that since submarine-launched missiles lack the accuracy of land-based intercontinental ballistic missiles (ICBMs), these surviving weapons could not be used against hardened Soviet silos but only against easy targets like cities. The American president would realize that to attack Soviet cities would probably cause the Soviets to launch their surviving missiles at American cities. Thus, the president's choices would be limited to suicide or surrender.

In this scenario, hawk strategists assumed that the Soviet leader was more willing than the American to risk mutual suicide, for they had the Russian launching the first attack but portrayed the American president as reluctant to counterattack. No doubt, Soviet hawks made similarly unflattering assumptions about American leaders. Dove strategists contended that the Soviets were no more likely than Americans to risk MAD.

The hawk scenario also assumed that the president must choose between launching all of his submarine missiles or none of them. But he could order a single submarine to retaliate against a limited number of targets, thus turning the tables on the Soviets. If they then fired at American cities, they would bring the remainder of the American submarine-launched missiles down on their own cities. These back-and-forth arguments illustrate the extremely hypothetical and value-laden grounds upon which nuclear strategy was built during the Cold War.

While the above scenario describes a breakdown of deterrence due to the development of offensive (first strike) weapons, the standoff can also be undermined by defensive means. Think again of our two men with revolvers held at each other's heads, but this time each one wears a bulletproof helmet. Now, protected from a fatal bullet to the head, neither has any strong restraint against wounding the other's body. Similarly, if the United States or the Soviet Union could have defended itself from a nuclear attack, it, too, might have been more willing to start a fight.

During the Cold War, the superpowers passed through phases of high and low interest in defenses against nuclear attack. In the 1950s and early 1960s, Americans participated in air raid drills and were encouraged to build fallout shelters. During the 1960s, both the Soviets and Americans developed systems to shoot down attacking ICBMs, but these were technically unsatisfactory. In signing the ABM treaty, both countries agreed to limit deployment of ABMs to insignificant levels.

Interest in missile defense reemerged in 1983 when President Reagan announced that the United States would begin development of a system to shield the American population from Soviet ICBMs. Dubbed "Star Wars" by the press, the proposed system depended on orbiting satellites for the immediate detection of a Soviet missile attack. Exotic weapons including lasers would destroy many of the attacking ICBMs within the first minutes after launch, while their booster rockets were still firing. Warheads that reached orbit would be destroyed by other weapons with the ability to discriminate them from the thousands of fake warheads that the Soviet ICBMs were expected to deploy as decoys. Any remaining warheads would be picked off by ABM rockets in the minutes before reaching their targets on American soil. The combined effect of these separate defensive tactics was projected to shield Americans from over 99 percent of the Soviet warheads so that damage from the few that hit would be at an acceptable level.

The Star Wars proposal quickly became controversial, partly because of its immense projected expense and partly because a large majority of American scientists regarded a shield that was 99 percent effective against a full Soviet missile attack to be technically unattainable. General Secretary Gorbachev of the Soviet Union strenuously objected to the Star Wars project, more so than to any other American weapons system, even refusing extensive arms control agreements because of it. This puzzled many Americans. Why should the Soviets object to a protective shield, especially one that probably wouldn't work?

Gorbachev's special concern over Star Wars was fully explicable if we consider its strategic implications from his viewpoint. It was irrelevant to him that the shield might be inadequate against a full Soviet attack if he had no expectation of ever launching such an attack. His greater worry was the possibility that America might attack the Soviet Union. In that case, Star Wars could give the United States a first-strike capability. A shield that might be too porous to stop the whole Soviet arsenal of missiles could work just fine against the fewer missiles surviving on submarines after a surprise American attack against Soviet silos and bomber bases. By protecting the Americans from Soviet retaliation, Star Wars would have made the USSR vulnerable to attack!

Today, the Soviet threat is over, but missile defense remains on the U.S. agenda, its present goal to protect Americans from attacks by the likes of North Korea or Iran. Between 1985 and 2004, over $80 billion was spent on development of Star Wars-like systems, and the expected cost over the period 2004–2009 exceeds $50 billion.

Critics of missile defense systems object on the grounds that these would destabilize mutual deterrence. Any rational adversary, fearing an American first-strike capability, would be under pressure to beef up its own strike capability, leading to an arms race. Furthermore, the critics argue, such "shields" can be overcome fairly easily. One of the cheapest ways is to build or buy small nuclear bombs—some fit into a suitcase—and smuggle them into the United States.

Happily, with the collapse of the Soviet Union, the threat of nuclear Armageddon disappeared, at least for the time being. We still face the threat of a nuclear detonation in one of our cities, perhaps sent by a terrorist or a "rogue state," but as horrible as this would be, it does not compare to 10,000 nuclear warheads striking at nearly the same time.

Conventional War

"Conventional war" refers to combat between national or guerilla armies using nonnuclear weapons. (Guerillas are soldiers who are not easily distinguished from civilians, relying less on uniforms and formal organization than does a regular army.) During 1990–2001, there were fifty-seven major armed conflicts in forty-five locations. These caused, according to the United Nations

(2003), 3.6 million deaths and many millions injured. More than 90 percent of casualties were civilians, and at least half were children, most of them hurt not by guns but by correlated famine or disruption. Sub-Saharan Africa was the hardest hit, but no region of the Third World was unaffected. Most of these wars, unless they involve Americans directly, are sparsely reported in the U.S. press. The Israeli-Palestinian conflict is the striking exception, receiving voluminous coverage by American journalists.

Unlike the world wars, which did indeed span much of the globe, wars since 1945 have normally been localized and have often been contained within a single country. While none of them can be understood without reference to the problems and politics of its particular place and time, we are more concerned here with common characteristics of these many conflicts, noting how they fit into a larger global pattern.

During the second half of the twentieth century, only a few wars were fought between industrialized nations, most prominently those pitting the Soviet Union against its satellites and those involving the disintegration of Yugoslavia. Nearly all of the other wars were fought on Third World soil, with the death and destruction falling overwhelmingly on poor people. When industrialized nations did became involved, they did not put their civilian populations at risk and were usually free to retire from combat at their choosing, without risk to their homelands.

To a considerable extent, governments of industrialized nations are free to choose where they want wars to occur, not so much by starting them in particular places as by choosing from among the many trouble spots around the world which ones to escalate into larger conflicts and which ones to discourage. This can be done by direct insertion or withdrawal of military forces, but it occurs more often by turning up or down the supply of arms and other material to local parties.

The situation in the Third World is different. Here, customary group identities based on tribal, ethnic, or religious differences remain important, perhaps increasingly so, judging from the current salience of fundamentalist religious identities. As the colonial empires broke up during the twentieth century, new nations were quickly constructed to fill the vacuum, usually under the guidance of the Western democracies. From 1945 to 1980, the number of independent countries grew from about 60 to 150. New national borders sometimes followed old colonial administrative boundaries that had little relevance for the indigenous people, perhaps splitting one tribe between two or more governments while encompassing competing or even hostile tribes under a single new government.

Each new nation needed an army, not only for defense but as a mark of sovereignty and prestige. The provision of quality equipment was an important way that political leaders maintained the support of their militaries. Usually, the people of these new nations lacked the traditions and material resources needed to support a stable democracy. Inevitably, there were clashes between those in power who favored their own groups and those who were left out or exploited. Dissidents often rebelled, and there were coups and civil wars aplenty.

For the departed colonial powers, these troubled new nations provided ample opportunities to reinsert themselves into the Third World. With Japan out of the action, the postwar competition was primarily between the Soviet and American blocs, which shifted their European competition into the new nations, especially in Asia, often using local armies as proxies to avoid a direct confrontation between the superpowers. Typically, America supported the government that had guided the new nation to power, while the Soviet Union supported the peasant rebels who justified their struggle in terms of Marxist ideology. With similar "wars of liberation" happening in so many places, it was easy to get the impression during the 1950s and 1960s that the communists were fomenting a world revolution against capitalism, which they probably were. In retrospect, it was erroneous to regard world communism as a monolithic conspiracy, as became clear when the Sino-Soviet split became visible in the 1960s, or as the sole source of violent conflict. Today, with the Soviet Union defunct, there are still plenty of wars raging around the globe.

The attacks of September 11, 2001, bringing death and destruction to Manhattan and Washington, were a conspicuous departure from the usual combat arenas in the Third World.

Subsequently, Russia and Spain suffered horrific strikes in their cities, and Israeli civilians are routinely targeted. It is too early to tell if these are anomalies, or if the cities of industrialized nations will more frequently become battlefields of the twenty-first century. In any case, Third World populations will likely continue to suffer the brunt of war. The American invasion of Afghanistan, a direct response to 9/11, and the subsequent American and British invasion of Iraq, allegedly another response to terrorism, have killed many more civilians than died on 9/11.

Terrorism

"Terrorism" is the illegitimate use of violence for political ends. Often, it is one of the few means available for groups with real grievances to challenge states with vastly superior military capability. It is easily distinguished from ordinary crimes of murder and kidnapping because terrorists always give a political motive for their actions, claiming to serve the greater good of some larger constituency, whereas ordinary criminals pursue only their own personal gains. The sanctioned use of violence by repressive governments to control their citizens is not usually counted as terrorism because it is "legal" by virtue of being official policy, although obviously the victims of "state terrorism" do not see it that way.

Sometimes it is difficult to differentiate terrorism from legitimate warfare. Often, guerillas are charged with terror tactics as a way of discrediting them when, in fact, their actions are little different from those of a regular army. Some of the fighting between Palestinians and Israelis, for example, is conventional guerilla warfare rather than terrorism. Terror, as distinct from terrorism, is a normal part of war. The soldiers of a nation are allowed, even required, to kill enemy soldiers. Judging from the actions of modern nations at war, soldiers may also be required to kill civilians, usually not as primary targets but in the process of attacking a clear military objective, as in the bombardment of a strategically important city. These actions are not generally regarded as crimes or terrorism, and usually soldiers are not held accountable for them after the war. The "war crimes" trials at Nuremberg after World War II were aimed at Nazi leaders and militarily irrelevant atrocities such as were committed by Hitler's special SS troops, not by the ordinary German soldier.

If the perpetrators of political violence are soldiers of an army representing a real constituency, and if they are in a recognized state of war with their victims' nation (whether formally declared or not), and if violence against civilians occurs as a reasonable by-product of attack against a clear military target, then these actions may be regarded as legitimate warfare rather than terrorism. However, such judgments are often ambiguous. Rashomon interpretations are especially likely in cases where a guerilla force of insurgents fights a regular state army. Naturally, a sitting government will regard any rebellion against it as illegal, while the rebels may regard themselves as a real people's army fighting a just war against oppression. Allies of the insurgents are more likely than their enemies to claim legitimacy for themselves and their actions.

"Terrorist" is a pejorative term applied only to our enemies, never to our friends, no matter how horribly they behave. It is sometimes used as a broad brush to tar all real or potential enemies, as in President George W. Bush's "War on Terrorism." During the insurgency following the 2003 war in Iraq, even insurgent attacks against superior-armed U.S. military convoys were labeled "terrorist."

The perception of terrorism is not wholly subjective, for there are instances when hardly anyone but the perpetrators themselves and their staunchest allies make a serious claim that their actions are legitimate. Few would quibble whether or not Osama bin Laden and his minions are terrorists. The dreadful attacks on crowded commuter trains in Madrid or on a Russian school filled with children, the suicide bombings of Israeli teenagers at a disco or shopping center, the humiliation and beheading of innocent civilians by Iraqi insurgents, the explosion at the Oklahoma City federal building perpetrated by Timothy McVeigh and Terry Nichols—these are unambiguously heinous actions to nearly everyone.

For as long as nations have shared common norms about the proper conduct of war, there have been terrorist violations; however, these increased noticeably after World War II in accompaniment to the guerilla wars and liberation movements in the Third World. Terrorism became especially intense during the 1970s within the context of the Arab-Israeli conflict, taking on its modern hallmarks of internationalism, state support, and intensive coverage in the mass media.

There was already a history of atrocities committed by both Jews and Arabs against each other when modern Israel was created in 1948. The birth of the new nation was greeted by the surrounding Arab nations with an immediate military attack. Many Arabs who had long lived in Israel (called "Palestine" since Roman times) fled to the attacking countries to escape the fighting. A bitter debate persists over the extent to which these people were encouraged to leave by Arab leaders versus being forced out by the Israelis. In any case, after winning the war, Israel did not allow them to return to their homes. Their Arab hosts enforced their resettlement into refugee camps near the borders of Israeli-occupied land, where many still live with their descendants. These Palestinians, who had not previously had much self-identity as a group, began to see themselves as particularly disadvantaged pawns of the opposing states but especially the victims of Israel.

The Six Day War of 1967 was a critical event because it demonstrated Israel's overwhelming military superiority over the humiliated Arab armies, dashing Palestinian hopes that they could win their homes back. To make matters worse, Israel won control of the West Bank of the Jordan River and Gaza, including the refugee camps set up there in 1948 by the United Nations to house the refugees who could neither return to Israel nor be admitted by neighboring Arab nations. In frustration, some of the Palestinians turned to terrorist tactics, including targets outside of Israel. Many of these acts received spectacular coverage in the mass media, especially the killing of eleven Israeli athletes at the 1972 Olympic Games in Munich. This visibility and the probable sponsorship of nations hostile to Israel or the United States—some of them newly rich with oil money—combined during the 1970s to foster the growth of global support networks. As a result, the previously existing level of terrorism intensified worldwide (Braungart and Braungart, 1983). Today's signature act—the suicide bombing—has distant precedents, but its modern phase began in the early 1980s with Iranian-backed Hezbollah in Lebanon and, among non-Muslims, the Tamil Tigers of Sri Lanka.

There is much speculation about the sort of person who becomes a terrorist. Like those who perform other kinds of violence, they tend to be young males, committed to their cause. Some argue that terrorists must be fanatics, even demented, to commit such inhumane acts. Others claim that most are essentially normal people who have become socialized into abnormal situations. The most daring or compliant of them follow orders from respected leaders to strike out at impersonal targets in ways that seem justifiable in that setting even though they appear inhumane to detached observers.

Remember that many acts of our enemies that we label as "terrorism" are in the perpetrators' eyes no different than conventional warfare is to us. The incentives for war discussed at the beginning of this chapter apply more or less to them as well. Ideological and religious motives are more important for the guerilla or terrorist than for the uniformed soldier who has little idea why he or she is sent to a foreign war. Certainly, the terrorist is more likely to be motivated by pure hatred, sometimes derived from firsthand experience with the oppressor. The formal command pyramid is more important for soldiers in a regular army than for terrorists who operate in small, relatively isolated groups. Perhaps among the strongest terrorist motives is to be someone, a man, a romantic hero, proud and admired as a brave warrior—an Achilles or Ivanhoe—who resists oppression and wreaks vengeance on the oppressor. A Muslim suicide bomber has the additional incentive of immediately entering Paradise after dying a martyr in the cause of holy war (jihad).

With the intense coverage given to terrorism in the world press, some, like Osama bin Laden, have become world-class heroes to their constituents. The media are a global stage for terrorists, televising statements or interviews with those holding civilian hostages. The Internet goes one better, even showing grisly beheadings. By giving these perpetrators fame and stature and by publicizing their grievances, media coverage helps the attackers mobilize followers and brings pressure to bear on the governments they hope to intimidate.

6

Inequality

"The big fish eat the little fish" is a maxim of international relations, meaning that powerful nations enforce their interests against weaker ones. This is not entirely true, since small nations often form coalitions to protect their interests against "big fish," and there are international conventions that constrain the use of raw power. Sometimes the "little fish" defend themselves with surprising effect, as the Americans learned in Vietnam and the Soviets in Afghanistan. Still, the nations that are most powerful militarily and economically tend to arrange international affairs to suit themselves.

That is what people usually mean when they speak of inequality in the world. We will pursue a different meaning of the term here since we are not especially interested in international politics but in global-level problems. Inequality for us means that people in some areas of the world live well, enjoying many material benefits and personal freedoms, while those living elsewhere have fewer or none of these advantages. Inequality in this sense is the most important global problem after the prevention of large-scale war.

Everyone knows that the United States and other industrial democracies—the "First World"—provide the richest and freest lives for most of their citizens, while some other countries are desperately impoverished or despotic or both. We need to add detail to this picture. In which areas of the Third World are lifestyles improving, and where are future prospects bleak? How bad is the plight of the former communist nations—in Cold War terms, the "Second World"—and how far have they moved toward democracy? Do prosperous nations spread benefits to all of their citizens?

How can the world become a better place to live for more of its people? The rich lifestyles of Japan and the West are based on very high and still increasing consumption of material things. This consumption is depleting limited resources and polluting the environment. Can we afford to have the rest of the world adopt our consumption styles? Can we afford to continue them ourselves?

Indicators of Material Lifestyle

Leaving aside personal freedom, there are material features of life that make it more or less pleasant to live. Besides the necessities of food, shelter, and clothing, one would like sanitary conditions and medical care, some education, secure employment, and entertainment. These are elements of a good life, whether one lives in a democracy or a dictatorship, under capitalism or communism, or in a secular society or a theocracy.

To assess the material lifestyles in different areas of the world, we require indicators of prosperity that are fairly well measured in most countries. One commonly used is gross domestic product (GDP), that is, the cash value of all finished goods and services produced in a nation in one year. Other things equal, nations with large populations have more economic activity than smaller nations, so to get a truer notion of the average citizen's prosperity, it is better to use GDP per capita, obtained by dividing each nation's GDP by its population size. This allows a fair comparison between, say, the enormous population of China and the medium-sized population of Italy. (Each nation's GDP must be converted to a common denominator, say euros, or U.S. dollars, or equivalent purchasing power.)

Besides economic measures, there are important health-related indicators. Infant mortality rate (i.e., the number of babies per thousand newborns who die before they are one year old) is a major factor in life expectancy. All parents want their babies to live, and everyone wants a long and healthy life for themselves. One might also measure adequacy of diet, access to safe water and sanitation, average number of people per household room, extent of schooling and literacy, number of TV sets per thousand people, and so on. Each indicator is narrow in scope and has methodological limitations, but they all tend to rank nations similarly, from those with the most comfortable material conditions to those with the poorest.

In 1990, the United Nations adopted the Human Development Index (HDI), a measure combining three dimensions of material well-being: life expectancy, adult literacy rate (and school enrollment), and GDP per capita. Since these dimensions are not expressed in the same unit, the HDI necessarily combines them in an arbitrary way, but nonetheless is a good summary measure. In 2001, Norway had the highest HDI of any nation (HDI = 0.944), while the United States was tied with Canada for seventh place (HDI = 0.937), and Sierra Leone in Africa ranked lowest (HDI = 0.275).

Rich Areas and Poor Areas

There are about 180 nations in the world, too many to keep track of, so we will focus on the fifty most populous countries—those with at least 18 million citizens. Although Afghanistan, North Korea, and Iraq each have 20–30 million people, they are excluded because up-to-date information is unavailable, either because of state secrecy (North Korea) or war-torn conditions (Afghanistan and Iraq). The fifty nations for which we do have current data contain nearly 90 percent of the world's population, so exclusions do not seriously distort our picture of global conditions.

Even fifty nations are too many to absorb, so we group them into eight clusters, each cluster reflecting common geographic or

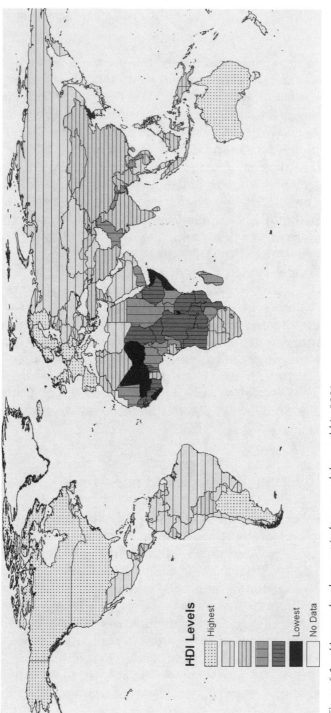

HDI Levels

Highest

Lowest

No Data

Figure 6.1.   Human development index around the world in 2001

cultural features. The first cluster, the **industrial democracies**, contains the largest countries of Western Europe, the United States, Canada, Japan, and Australia. Perhaps more surprising is the inclusion of Poland, Romania, and South Korea. Poland, largest of the westernmost nations that broke from the former Soviet bloc in 1989–1991, is now a democracy and a member of NATO and the European Union. Romania, another former Soviet satellite nation, is scheduled to join the EU in 2007. (Formerly communist East Germany is now part of Germany.) South Korea developed rapidly after the Korean War (1950–1953), first economically and then democratically, becoming one of the few nations to leap the gap between the Third and First Worlds. (Taiwan is another, but following UN practice, its 22 million people are here included as part of China.)

Table 6.1 shows the nations in each cluster, arranged alphabetically. Column 1 gives each nation's HDI score for 2001 plus each cluster's average HDI (weighted by population) in boldface. These scores show that life in the industrial democracies is materially better than elsewhere—this is no surprise. Even Poland, its HDI = 0.84, ranks high compared to the rest of the world. Only Romania (HDI = 0.77) lags considerably behind.

Column 2 shows the percentage change in HDI from 1990 to 2001. (Statisticians will frown at calculating percentages for ordinal measurements, but this is justifiable for present purposes.) On average, HDI in the industrial democracies improved modestly (+3 percent) over that period, but not much more could be expected since most of these nations already had high life expectancy, literacy, and GDP per capita.

Column 3 shows the percentage of each nation's population living in urban areas. These are very high in the industrialized democracies, averaging 79 percent in contrast to agrarian societies where people still live mostly in rural areas.

Until the collapse of the Soviet Union, its industrialized components were running second behind the Western democracies in material lifestyle and well ahead of the Third World. After the disintegration, most of the former satellite nations (and the Baltic republics of the former USSR) turned westward, leaving the eastern components in meltdown. Twelve of the fifteen former republics of the USSR joined to form a loose Commonwealth of Independent States (CIS). I limit the second cluster in table 6.1, labeled **former Soviet Union**, to the largest fragments of the CIS: Russia, Ukraine, and Uzbekistan. They have suffered badly since the breakup, as reflected in an average *decline* (-4%) in HDI from 1990 to 2001. The situation seems to have improved since 2001, and we may see an upturn in the coming decades. But for the moment, the former Soviet Union can no longer claim a lifestyle superior to every region of the Third World.

From the perspective of the industrial democracies, material life everywhere else is simply deficient, but this is an inadequate judgment because it ignores the wide differences that exist across other parts of the globe. To examine the Third World in greater detail, I sort its larger nations into six clusters on the basis of geographic contiguity and cultural similarity. These clusters are Latin America, the Middle East, China, Southeast Asia, South Asia, and Sub-Saharan Africa.

Latin America, stretching from Mexico to the southern tip of South America, was colonized by Spain and Portugal. Today, it is mostly Catholic and Spanish-speaking (though Brazilians speak Portuguese). Overall, Latin America is the most prosperous region of the Third World, with HDI scores of its large nations ranging from 0.75 to 0.85, higher than the former Soviet Union. The average improvement in HDI from 1990 to 2001 was a respectable +6 percent. This statistical picture is somewhat misleading because it overlooks the smaller nations of Central America, some of them extremely poor, and ignores the huge urban slums of Latin American cities. Still, Latin America is more developed and its nations are more urban (averaging 79 percent) than other large regions of the Third World.

The **Middle East** includes the Muslim nations of southwest Asia and northern Africa. Most of these are Arab regimes, their people speaking Arabic and sharing a group identity with other Arabs. Non-Arab Iran and Turkey are important exceptions. Much of the region was under Ottoman Turk rule until the end of World War I, and much was under British and French control before gaining independence in the mid-twentieth century. Most

Table 6.1. Development indicators for fifty nations

	1. HDI in 2001	2. Percent Change in HDI 1990 to 2001	3. Percent Urban in 2001	4. Rating of Civil Rights in 2004	5. Income Inequality: Richest 10% to poorest 10%	6. Ratio of Female to Male literacy, 2001
Industrial Democracies	**0.93**	**3**	**79**	**1.0**	**12.3**	**–**
Australia	0.94	6	91	1	12.5	–
Canada	0.94	1	79	1	9.0	–
France	0.93	3	76	1	9.1	–
Germany	0.92	4	78	1	14.2	–
Italy	0.92	4	67	1	14.5	0.99
Japan	0.93	3	79	1	4.5	–
Poland	0.84	6	63	1	7.8	.00
Romania	0.77	1	55	1	7.2	0.98
South Korea	0.88	8	82	1	7.8	0.97
Spain	0.92	4	78	1	9.0	0.98
United Kingdom	0.93	6	90	1	13.4	–
United States	0.94	3	77	1	16.6	–
Former Soviet Union	**0.78**	**–4**	**67**	**2.1**	**15.5**	**1.00**
Russia	0.78	–4	73	2	20.3	.00
Ukraine	0.77	–4	68	2	6.4	.00
Uzbekistan	0.73	0	37	3	6.1	0.99

(continued)

Table 6.1. (*continued*)

	1. HDI in 2001	2. Percent Change in HDI 1990 to 2001	3. Percent Urban in 2001	4. Rating of Civil Rights in 2004	5. Income Inequality: Richest 10% to poorest 10%	6. Ratio of Female to Male literacy, 2001
Latin America	**0.81**	**6**	**79**	**1.1**	**50.1**	**0.98**
Argentina	0.85	5	88	1	-	1.00
Brazil	0.78	9	82	1	65.8	1.00
Colombia	0.78	-4	76	2	42.7	1.00
Mexico	0.8	6	75	1	34.6	0.96
Peru	0.75	7	73	1	22.3	0.90
Venezuela	0.78	3	87	1	44.0	0.99
Middle East	**0.67**	**11**	**57**	**2.6**	**12**	**0.74**
Algeria	0.70	9	58	3	9.6	0.76
Egypt	0.65	13	43	3	8.0	0.67
Iran	0.72	11	65	3	17.2	0.84
Morocco	0.61	13	56	2	11.7	0.59
Saudi Arabia	0.77	7	87	3	-	0.82
Turkey	0.73	8	66	2	13.3	0.82
Yemen	0.47	20	25	2	8.6	0.39
China	**0.72**	**16**	**37**	**3**	**12.7**	**0.85**
Southeast Asia	**0.70**	**10**	**39**	**2**	**22**	**0.95**
Indonesia	0.68	10	42	2	7.8	0.90
Malaysia	0.79	10	58	2	22.1	0.92

Myanmar (Burma)	0.55	-	28	3	-	0.91
Philippines	0.75	5	59	1	16.5	1.00
Thailand	0.77	7	20	1	13.4	0.97
Vietnam	0.69	14	25	3	8.4	0.96
South Asia	**0.57**	**14**	**28**	**1.4**	**8.9**	**0.65**
Bangladesh	0.50	21	26	2	6.8	0.62
India	0.59	14	28	1	9.5	0.67
Nepal	0.50	21	12	2	9.3	0.42
Pakistan	0.50	13	33	3	7.6	0.49
Sri Lanka	0.73	6	23	2	7.9	0.94
Sub-Saharan Africa	**0.45**	**6**	**36**	**2**	**31.6**	**0.76**
Congo, Dem. Rep.	0.36	–13	-	3	-	0.70
Ethiopia	0.31	18	16	2	59.7	0.67
Ghana	0.57	10	36	1	14.1	0.80
Kenya	0.49	–9	34	2	15.6	0.86
Mozambique	0.36	12	33	2	12.5	0.49
Nigeria	0.46	9	45	2	24.9	0.79
South Africa	0.68	–7	58	1	65.1	0.98
Sudan	0.50	17	37	3	-	0.68
Tanzania	0.40	–2	33	2	10.8	0.80
Uganda	0.49	21	15	2	9.9	0.74

Sources: United Nations Development Programme, *Human Development Report 2003*, Freedom House, *Freedom of the World 2004*

Middle Eastern nations (but not Turkey) are united by antipathy of varying degrees toward the Jewish state of Israel in their midst.

The Middle Eastern nations are importantly divided into those with large oil deposits (Saudi Arabia, Iran, Iraq, and Algeria) and those without (Egypt, Morocco, Turkey, and Yemen). The oil nations, united under the Organization of Petroleum Exporting Countries (OPEC), along with non-Arab oil producers Venezuela, Nigeria, and Indonesia, have since the 1970s greatly increased their revenues compared to their poor neighbors. Some countries too small for our list—Qatar and the United Arab Emirates—have attained the highest per capita GDPs in the world, yet the region as a whole remains underdeveloped and is ruled by monarchs and strongmen. During the 1980s, Iran and Iraq wasted much of their oil money and a half million lives on a stalemated war against one another. Subsequently, the United States went to war twice in Iraq.

In 2001, the average HDI for Middle Eastern nations was 0.67, which is middling compared to the rest of the Third World. There is much variation within the region. In 2001, fabulously oil-rich Saudi Arabia had an HDI of 0.77, while impoverished Yemen's HDI was 0.47, and that after a decade of rapid improvement. Overall, HDI in the Middle East improved at a good clip (+11 percent) between 1990 and 2001, but considering all of the oil money flowing there, many regard this as a disappointing performance.

One-fifth of the world's population lives in **China**. That, plus China's phenomenal economic gains during the past decades, earn it a cluster of its own. From 1990 to 2001, China's Human Development Index improved a blistering +16 percent, giving it in 2001 an HDI of 0.72. While far below Latin America, this was much better than China's desperate condition under Maoist rule and good compared to much of the Third World. It is important to note, however, that China remains primarily an agrarian nation. In 2001, only 37 percent of Chinese lived in cities, where the new prosperity is occurring. In the countryside, most people remain poor. There are now billionaires in this nominally communist nation, while hordes of people still live hard lives—a situation fertile for discontent.

The cluster of nations in **Southeast Asia** is a mixed bag linguistically, religiously, racially, and politically. Their main point in common is geography, but even here they divide into peninsular Asia (Myanmar, Thailand, and Vietnam) and island nations (Indonesia and the Philippines). Average 2001 HDI = 0.70 for this cluster, nearly the same as in China. Between 1990 and 2001, HDI increased +10 percent, a decent improvement but not up to China's fast pace.

We turn finally to two regions of the globe where the material conditions of day-to-day life—even in peacetime—are most miserable. One is **South Asia**, a cluster of mostly populous Muslim, Hindu, and Buddhist nations. The largest of these is India, containing one-sixth of the world's population. Also included are Pakistan and Bangladesh, which broke from India when it gained independence from Britain after World War II. For South Asia as a whole, HDI in 2001 was 0.57, a very low level. On the bright side, most of these nations saw high rates of improvement (from very low bases) between 1990 and 2001. South Asia remains mostly agrarian, with only 28 percent of its population urbanized in 2001.

The most desperately unfortunate region of the world is **Sub-Saharan Africa**, or "black Africa." It contains a mixture of languages, religions, and tribes. Many of these nations were colonized by Europeans during the scramble for African possessions in the nineteenth century; most became independent after World War II and are or have been badly governed and corrupt. This is the most AIDS-infected region of the world and is the area least able to afford medication. In 2001, Sub-Saharan Africa's average HDI was 0.45, the lowest of any major region. Individual nations score as low as Ethiopia (HDI = 0.31) and as high as South Africa (HDI = 0.68). There is a mostly black government in today's South Africa, and racial discrimination is illegal, but South African whites still live in comfortable isolation from the majority of poor blacks, so the nation's HDI understates the situation of the white population and overstates the well-being of blacks.

In December 2004, a giant tsunami struck the densely populated nations bordering the Indian Ocean, causing unprecedented loss of life from a natural disaster, especially in Indonesia, Sri Lanka, Thailand, and India. One more misfortune piled atop others.

Human Rights

People do not live by bread alone; nurturing the human spirit is also important. The tenets of liberal democracy are that all people should have a say in how they are governed, should elect their leaders, and in order to do so should have free access to truthful information, including an uncensored press. People should have freedom of action as long as it does not impinge on others, freedom of belief and of speech, and they should be protected against criminal prosecution without due legal process, including the right to a fair trial. They should be free to assemble in public for purposes of discussion or to promote courses of action. These are the political and civil rights stated in the U.S. Constitution and its Bill of Rights. There have been serious lapses from these formal guarantees, especially involving racial discrimination—including the appalling treatment of American Indians, the internment of American citizens of Japanese descent during World War II, and "Jim Crow" laws discriminating against blacks prior to the civil rights reforms of the 1960s. Overall, however, political and civil rights operate remarkably well for citizens of the United States and the other industrial democracies. How well do they operate in the rest of the world?

This is a harder question than our inquiry about material lifestyle because human rights are not as easily measured as GDP or literacy rate. Amnesty International and other nongovernmental organizations, as well as the United Nations, issue frequent reports on human rights around the world, but usually these do not give simple ratings that facilitate international comparisons. Furthermore, the ideology of liberal democracy, with its emphasis on individual freedom, is a Western invention, and there is no reason to expect those from other cultural traditions to value it highly.

Despite these problems, it is worthwhile comparing our version of human rights—civil rights—in different regions of the world. For this, I use evaluations from Freedom House, a conservative American group known for its capsule ratings of nations as free, partly free, and not free. Freedom House ratings are in good agreement with summary ratings from other credible sources (Taylor and Jodice, 1983; Humana, 1986), and they have the advantage of being as recent as 2004.

Roughly speaking, a nation is called "free" (and scored 1) when the great majority of its people have the right and opportunity to elect political leaders, political parties may be freely formed to compete for office, and a leader or party can indeed be voted out of office. Furthermore, the rule of law is binding, and there is free expression including an uncensored press. In practice, these rights may not be fully realized because of violence, poverty, or unavailability of the media. Nations called "not free" (and scored 3) have no elections, or elections that involve only a single list of candidates, and individuals' civil rights are not protected over the priorities of the state. The designation "partly free" (scored 2) is intermediate between these extremes. Freedom House ratings for 2004 are shown in column 4 of table 6.1.

The industrial democracies all rate 1.0 on civil rights. (Freedom House makes finer distinctions and does not regard Japan or the novices in this cluster—Poland, Romania, and South Korea—as free as the Western democracies.) The remnants of the former Soviet Union averaged 2.1 in 2004, an improvement since the old USSR but not yet Western-style democracy. At the end of 2004, public protests in Ukraine over a flawed election unseated the illegally "elected" pro-Russian prime minister and forced a new, more honest vote. Perhaps this marks a new liberalization in post-Soviet politics.

Latin America contains some of the freest citizens in the Third World, its larger nations averaging 1.1 on civil rights. The dictatorships of a few decades ago are gone from the large nations. Some smaller countries of Latin America, not on the list, still have severe problems with civil rights, notably Haiti and Cuba.

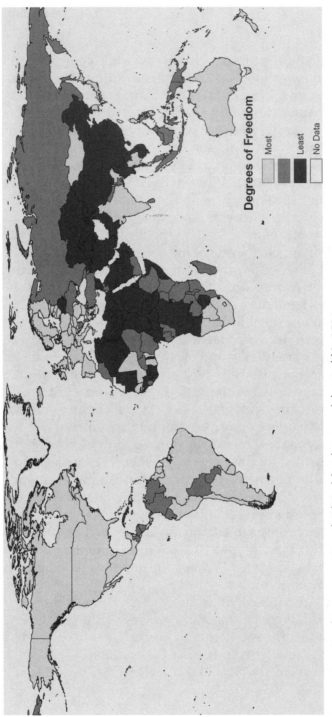

Degrees of Freedom

Most

Least

No Data

Figure 6.2.   Freedom House rating of political freedom round the world in 2004

The mean score of 1.4 in South Asia indicates freedom nearly comparable to Latin America. This average is heavily weighted by India, the world's largest democracy, which is unusually free compared to other nations in the region. We see a similar mix in Southeast Asia: the Philippines and Thailand are free, while Myanmar (Burma) has a terrible record on liberty. Overall, Southeast Asia averages 2.0 on civil rights.

The irony of Sub-Saharan Africa is that South Africa, for years a pariah for the apartheid policy of its white rulers, is today a bastion of African civil rights. Unfortunately, official racism remains in other African nations where the oppressors are black. The average Freedom House score for Sub-Saharan Africa is 2.0.

The Middle East has no free nations (except little Israel, which, despite its geographical proximity, does not fit this cluster). The region's overall stance on civil rights is poor, averaging 2.6. Some of America's closest partners in the region, Saudi Arabia and Egypt, are among the worst offenders. The Middle East is desperately in need of political reform (Lewis, 2002). Perhaps Iraq will one day fulfill President George W. Bush's dream of a fully democratic Arab nation. A better bet may be Palestine, if it can make peace with Israel. Turkey, a Muslim but not an Arab state, is likely to continue liberalizing its politics as it seeks entry into the European Union.

Of all the clusters, China ranks lowest on civil rights. China is still nominally communist despite its capitalist economy, and the Party retains command of the nation, although it is a gentler totalitarianism than under Mao. Some observers predict that political freedom will follow the freeing-up of the economy.

Equity

Americans regarded the Soviet Union and other communist regimes as having an unacceptable posture toward civil rights. At the same time, the Soviets faulted America's record on human rights. Recalling Rashomon, we may try to understand these contradictory viewpoints by distinguishing two kinds of human rights: civil and economic. By "civil rights" we mean the traditional American freedoms of speech, religion, press, right of assembly, and freely elected government—those discussed in the previous section. "Economic rights" are the entitlement of people to feed, clothe, and provide material security for themselves and their families, free from the fear that this support might disappear. Following Karl Marx's idea that everyone in a nation has an equal claim on its benefits—that there should be no separation between the privileged rich and the exploited poor—the Soviets granted economic rights to all its citizens, claiming that these are as important as civil rights, perhaps more so since hungry people rarely worry about freedoms of speech or press until they have enough to eat. Every Soviet citizen was guaranteed a job, health care, and the basic means to support his or her family.

In theory, unemployment and poverty were eliminated from communist society; people could not suddenly find themselves out of work without money to care for their families, as occurs in the United States. The Soviets saw America's black and Hispanic slums, rife with crime, violence, and drug addiction, as the inevitable refuse of an "immoral system of free enterprise." Theoretically, the communist system had no such underclass, no victims of capitalist exploitation.

In fact, no communist society, and certainly not the Soviet Union, was without poverty. Soviet sources finally acknowledged that more than 20 percent of the population lived on less than 300 rubles a month for a family of four, which was the unofficial level of income needed to maintain "minimum material security." At the same time, political and professional elites lived relatively luxurious lives with access to special stores that stocked scarce consumer items (Smith, 1976). Today, with communism limited to China, North Korea, and Cuba, we may ask how the world is managing the problem of equal access to resources.

Turning again to our clusters of nations, we can examine their degree of equity, the extent to which economic rights or opportunities are distributed equally throughout a country's citizenry (United Nations, 2003). Think of the total income earned by all of a nation's citizens in one year as a pie. Imagine that one slice of the pie represents the income earned by the lowest-paid (poorest) 10 percent of workers. Another slice represents the income of the highest-paid (richest) 10 percent of citizens—this second piece is larger. (The rest of the pie represents all income going to the 80 percent of citizens whose earnings are in the middle.) By comparing the slices of the richest and poorest earners (i.e., calculating their ratio), we get a measure of the distribution of income. The higher the ratio, the more unequally the pie is shared.

Column 5 of table 6.1 shows, for each nation, the ratio of income going to the richest (highest 10 percent) versus the poorest (lowest 10 percent) earners during the 1990s. In the industrial democracies, the richest earners made 12.3 times as much money as the poorest earners. This distribution of income was not much different than in the former Soviet Union, or in China. We see no legacy here of Karl Marx's hope that workers under communism would share their society's rewards more equally than workers in capitalist societies.

If Marx were alive, he certainly would call for a revolution in Latin America, which has the most unequal distribution of income in the world. Here, the richest earners made fifty times more than the poorest earners! This helps explain an enigma: On the one hand, statistics show Latin America to be materially the most advanced area of the Third World, yet on the other hand, the region has so many poor people, especially in the sprawling slums of its large cities. How can both be true? The answer is that the region's considerable prosperity is poorly distributed. Latin Americans of European ancestry make far more money than those of Indian or mixed ancestry. In no other large (multinational) region of the world is inequity so stark. Although not shown in our statistics, there is also great inequality in the ownership of land in Latin America, with a relatively few families holding vast acreage.

Sub-Saharan Africa also had a skewed distribution of income, not as bad as Latin America, but still, the richest Africans made over thirty times as much as the poorest during the 1990s. To be poor in black Africa is to be absolutely poor. In contrast, South Asia had the least inequality in income distribution, with its richest people earning less than nine times the amount earned by its poorest. Here, at least, the misery is shared fairly equally.

Column 6 measures a different kind of equity, that between the sexes. As a crude indicator, we take the ratio of female adult literacy over male adult literacy. The closer this ratio is to 1.0, the more equal the sexes are in literacy.

The ratio is not calculated for most industrial democracies because gender equality (in literacy) is generally assumed. Column 6 shows sexual equality, or nearly so, in the former Soviet Union, Latin America, and Southeast Asia. In China, the ratio drops to 0.85. It is lower yet in the Middle East (0.74) and Sub-Saharan Africa (0.76). South Asia shows the worst inequity for females, its ratio a low 0.65. Full access to literacy is the smallest step toward gender equality. Once that is accomplished, there are many steps ahead.

Overview

The broad regions of the globe where life is materially poorest are Sub-Saharan Africa and South Asia. Supplementary data show that nations in these two clusters, with a few exceptions, have the least economic strength, the highest infant mortality, the least adequate diets, crowded housing, the least education, and few of the benefits of modern technology. In most, women are inferior to men, as reflected in low female literacy (compared to males). South Asia is improving, but some nations of Sub-Saharan Africa are worsening. On top of black Africa's old problems, the spread of AIDS is taking a terrible toll. Few governments in these areas offer their citizens true civil rights, the large exceptions being democratic India, South Africa, and Ghana. South Asia and Sub-Saharan Africa most desperately need help from the richer nations of the Northern Hemisphere.

Latin America is the region of the Third World where average material lifestyle is highest, where democratic governments are the most free, and the status of women is best. The great problem for Latin America is its grossly unequal distribution of wealth. While its richest citizens enjoy comfortable lifestyles and own most of the land, the poorest live in appalling slums. Latin America can help itself by instituting a more equitable distribution of its plentiful resources.

China, with one-fifth of the world's people, is growing economically at breakneck speed, while improvement in civil rights moves at a snail's pace. Despite being a communist nation, where citizens are supposed to share equally, China's distribution of income barely differs from that of the capitalist industrial democracies. There is a stark difference between affluent portions of its larger cities and continuing poverty in the countryside, where most people live. Not surprisingly, rural people are moving in large numbers to the cities. China, more than any other region, is riding the proverbial tiger, trying to maximize its gains without falling off and being eaten.

The oil-rich nations of the Middle East are most notable for their lost opportunities. While they have seen some improvement in material lifestyle, repressive governments have failed to deliver the degree of improvement that ought to have accompanied the huge stream of oil revenue flowing into the region. There is little progress in equalizing the status of women, a resource available even to the oil-poor nations of the area.

The cluster that has changed most since the first edition of this book is the former Soviet empire, including its industrial satellite nations of eastern Europe. In its heyday—the 1970s and 1980s—the Soviet bloc could claim a material lifestyle second only to the industrial democracies. Politically, of course, it was repressive. Faltering lifestyle during the 1990s was a contributor to the Soviet collapse, and conditions nose-dived after the breakup. The westernmost former satellites and the Baltic republics have joined the European Union, leaving Russia, Ukraine, and Uzbekistan as the major remnants of the old system. Although (mostly) politically freer, these nations have seen their economies collapse, leaving many citizens yearning for the old days. There are now signs of revival, too recent to show in table 6.1. If it is reinvigorated, Russia could again be a giant power. It is essential that it remains on peaceful terms with the West.

The gold medal for material lifestyle and for political and civil freedoms goes to the industrial democracies; we knew that all along. But the prize has some tarnish, for as long as nations as rich as these allow deep pockets of poverty and suffering to exist alongside conspicuous opulence, they cannot claim to have reached an admirable state of equity.

Can we realistically hope to raise everyone's material lifestyle to the level enjoyed today by Americans, Europeans, and Japanese? In some ways we probably can. Infant mortality around the world has dropped considerably since World War II and is still declining. Further improvement in sanitation, nutrition, and medical care—including drugs to fight AIDS—can allow nearly all babies to survive into adulthood.

In other ways, especially in consumption of energy and manufactured products, it would be very difficult, probably impossible, to bring everyone up to Western levels. Although Americans are only 5 percent of the world's population, we use 15 percent of the steel produced each year, 25 percent of the electricity, and 40 percent of the cars on the road. If all nations consumed at this level, it would be necessary to triple the world production of steel, generate five times the amount of electricity, and increase the manufacture of automobiles eightfold. This would place heavy demands on natural resources, driving their prices upward. The vastly increased scale of production and consumption would spew correspondingly higher quantities of refuse and other pollutants, degrading the environment and making it increasingly hazardous to health. These are heavy costs that may not be bearable.

What are the options? One way is to hold the rest of the world to a lower level of consumption, keeping our privileged position of affluence. Another is to reduce our own consumption—especially when it is wasteful, frivolous, or conspicuously Trumpian—so that worldwide equity is a more attainable goal. Many analysts claim that we could reduce consumption without much loss in the quality of our lives and that we would gain new benefits in the process. In chapter 8, we will consider again if people need to consume so much, but first we must understand why there are so many consumers.

7

Population

In 1950, there were roughly 2.5 billion people in the world, in 1990 about 5 billion, and in 2006 around 6.5 billion. The populations of most industrialized democracies are nearly stable, and the former Soviet Union is losing population, so this rapid increase is occurring almost entirely in the Third World.

Table 7.1 displays population characteristics of the fifty most populous nations, again divided into the eight clusters defined in chapter 6. Column 2 shows that between 1975 and 2001, population in the average industrial democracies increased only 0.7 percent yearly. By 2004, the average yearly increase was down to 0.5 percent.

Population increase (or decrease) depends not only on the balance between births and deaths, but also on the extent of in- or out-migration. In the United States, for example, population grew about 1 percent yearly during the last quarter of the twentieth century. Half of that increase was due to an excess of births over deaths, and half was due to the large number of immigrants moving to the United States, mostly from Third World nations.

Column 3 shows each nation's total fertility (per woman), that is, the average number of babies a woman will have during her lifetime. To maintain a constant population requires at least two births per woman (plus a slight excess to make up for females who die before reaching the age of childbearing). In

Table 7.1. Population, growth rate, and fertility

	1. Population (millions) 2001	2. Annual Percentage Population Growth		3. Total Fertility Rate (per Woman)	
		1975– 2001	2004	1970– 1975	2000– 2005
Industrial Democracies	**87**	**0.7**	**0.5**	**2.4**	**1.7**
Australia	19	1.3	0.9	2.5	1.7
Canada	31	1.1	0.9	2.0	1.5
France	60	0.5	0.4	2.3	1.9
Germany	82	0.5	0.0	2.9	1.2
Italy	58	0.1	0.1	2.3	1.2
Japan	127	0.5	0.1	2.1	1.3
Poland	39	0.5	0.0	2.3	1.3
Romania	22	0.2	−0.1	2.6	1.3
South Korea	47	1.1	0.6	4.3	1.4
Spain	41	0.5	0.2	2.9	1.2
United Kingdom	59	0.2	0.3	2.0	1.6
United States	288	1.0	0.9	2.0	2.1
Former Soviet Union	**219**	**-**	**−0.3**	**2.5**	**1.6**
Russia	145	0.3	−0.5	2.0	1.0
Ukraine	49	-	−0.7	2.2	1.2
Uzbekistan	25	2.3	1.7	6.3	2.4
Latin America	**407**	**1.9**	**1.2**	**5.1**	**2.4**
Argentina	38	1.4	1.0	3.1	2.4
Brazil	174	1.8	1.1	4.7	2.2
Colombia	43	2.0	1.5	5.0	2.6
Mexico	101	2.0	1.2	6.5	2.5
Peru	26	2.1	1.4	6.0	2.9
Venezuela	25	2.6	1.4	4.9	2.7
Middle East	**308**	**2.5**	**1.5**	**6.2**	**3.0**
Algeria	31	2.5	1.3	7.4	2.8
Egypt	69	2.2	1.8	5.7	3.3
Iran	67	2.7	1.1	6.4	2.3
Morocco	30	2.1	1.6	6.9	2.7
Saudi Arabia	23	4.4	2.4	7.3	4.5
Turkey	69	2.0	1.1	5.2	2.4
Yemen	19	3.8	3.4	8.4	7.0
China	**1,285**	**1.3**	**0.6**	**4.9**	**1.8**

	1. Population (millions) 2001	2. Annual Percentage Population Growth		3. Total Fertility Rate (per Woman)	
		1975– 2001	2004	1970– 1975	2000– 2005
Southeast Asia	**504**	**1.9**	**1.4**	**5.7**	**2.6**
Indonesia	214	1.8	1.5	5.2	2.4
Malaysia	24	2.5	1.8	5.2	2.9
Myanmar (Burma)	48	1.8	0.5	5.8	2.9
Philippines	77	2.3	1.9	6.0	3.2
Thailand	62	1.5	0.9	5.0	1.9
Vietnam	79	1.9	1.3	6.7	2.3
South Asia	**1,363**	**2.1**	**1.5**	**5.6**	**3.3**
Bangladesh	141	2.4	2.1	6.2	3.5
India	1,033	2.0	1.4	5.4	3.0
Nepal	24	2.3	2.2	5.8	4.3
Pakistan	146	2.8	2.0	6.3	5.1
Sri Lanka	19	1.3	0.8	4.1	2.0
Sub-Saharan Africa	**440**	**2.8**	**2.0**	**6.8**	**5.4**
Congo, Dem. Rep.	50	2.8	3.0	6.5	6.7
Ethiopia	67	2.7	1.9	6.8	6.1
Ghana	20	2.7	1.4	6.9	4.1
Kenya	31	3.2	1.1	8.1	4.0
Mozambique	18	2.1	1.2	6.6	5.6
Nigeria	118	2.9	2.5	6.9	5.4
South Africa	44	2.1	−0.3	5.4	2.6
Sudan	32	2.5	2.6	6.7	4.4
Tanzania	36	3.0	2.0	6.8	6.7
Uganda	24	3.1	3.0	7.1	7.1

Sources: UN Development Program, *Human Development Report 2003*; CIA, *World Factbook 2004*.

the period 1970–1975, the average American woman had two babies—approximately the "replacement" level. At that time, most other industrial democracies had higher fertility than the United States. But by 2000–2005 there was a reversal. U.S. fertility rose slightly, to 2.1 babies per woman. Fertility in all other industrial democracies has dropped sharply—to well below the replacement level.

Population decline is most pronounced in the former Soviet Union. During the last decades of the empire's existence, population was fairly level. After the Soviet collapse, population declined in earnest. By 2004, this cluster was losing 0.3 percent of its population (column 2). During the period 2000–2005, the average Russian woman was having only one baby during her lifetime (column 3). Population decline was reinforced by an increase in infant mortality and a decrease in overall life expectancy.

All of the Third World clusters have higher population growth rates, and higher fertility rates, than the stable industrial democracies or the declining former Soviet Union (table 7.1). Since the Third World comprises 80 percent of the Earth's people, even a small percentage increase adds a lot of people each year.

Malthus

The notion that human population would rise so fast as to outstrip its food supply was popularized by the Reverend Thomas Malthus. Writing in Britain in 1798, as that country was beginning to industrialize, Malthus was struck by the rapid population growth at home and especially in America. He warned of inevitable calamity unless growth could be slowed. Reflecting the religious morality of his time, Malthus advocated sexual abstinence, a solution as unrealistic in his day as in our own.

A simple "Malthusian" version of the global population problem is widely accepted today. It holds that the entire world is overpopulated, that there is not enough food for the people already here, that continued population growth will cause worldwide starvation, and that it is therefore imperative for families and nations everywhere to limit new births to a degree that there is zero increase or even decline in population. If readers come to this chapter with that view, my main purpose will be to convince them that these are not the essential features of the world's population problem. This simplistic view ignores some of the really tragic aspects of the problem, and it distracts our attention from important possibilities for solution.

There will be no worldwide starvation in the foreseeable future. Given the extreme inequalities of wealth and power among nations, it is clear that hunger will be restricted to the poorer nations and to poverty pockets of the wealthier ones, which has been true for years. The well-to-do usually have enough to eat even while the poor go hungry, as Malthus himself noted, and there is no reason to think that this pattern will change.

It is unclear if the world as a whole is overpopulated, at least in any way that experts would agree about. All do agree that many Third World nations like China and India have too many people by any reasonable standard, but few experts would say that about the United States with its slowly growing population (about 1 percent per year), so rich in food-producing resources that farmers grow less than they could. It is difficult to combine such diverse situations in individual countries into an aggregate judgment that the world as a whole is overpopulated. Any such claim must be subjective and uncertain because no one knows the ultimate food-producing capacity of the Earth, which depends not only on countable assets like the acreage of arable land but also on intangibles such as the quality of agricultural technology (including genetically modified crops) that will be available in the future.

By overemphasizing number of people as the cause of starvation, we are distracted from other causes that may be more pressing and easier to correct. Today, there is enough food in the world to feed everyone adequately, and food supply is increasing faster than population. Yet about 10 percent of the world's population suffers from serious malnutrition, and there are still instances of mass starvation in Africa or Asia. This situation is not markedly different from what it was in 1990 when the world had 1.5 billion fewer people. The number of people is not the essential problem here as much as our inability to distribute existing food to the people who need it. During some of the worst recent instances of mass starvation in Ethiopia, Somalia, and Sudan, food shipments went undelivered to victims because they could not cross the battle lines drawn by civil war (Perlez, 1988).

More often, food fails to reach hungry people because they are poor and cannot afford it.

Certainly, it is imperative for governments of rapidly growing nations with strained resources to encourage limits for their populations, but that may not be a desirable policy for countries that already have fairly stable or declining populations, which includes most of Europe and Japan. Some of these nations fear that they will not have enough citizens to fill jobs needed for expanding economies or for a sufficient workforce to support government-sponsored retirement programs (like Social Security).

The world's population during the twenty-first century would be little different if all Americans, Japanese, and Europeans limited themselves to two children, as some have advocated, because over 90 percent of the global increase in population is coming from the Third World. Americans would help the world more by increasing our production of truly useful goods and by curtailing our obscene waste than by further limiting the size of our already small families.

Population during the Great Transformations

We have only crude estimates of the size of world population for any time more than a century ago. It seems from archaeological remains that the "human" population of the genus *Homo* grew slowly during most of its 2 million years of existence on earth. About 10,000 years ago, near the beginning of the Agrarian/Urban Transformation, population increased far more than it had before as people began to concentrate in towns and cities, living off crops and livestock raised nearby. We cannot say if this unprecedented increase in human numbers was a cause or a consequence of agrarian life, but there is no doubt that these changes are intimately connected (chapter 2).

Human population began a second unprecedented increase less than 400 years ago. Like most agrarian societies, those of the time had high birthrates, of the order of thirty to fifty births per thousand population per year (Hauser, 1979; Weeks, 1986). With preindustrial death rates (yearly deaths per thousand population) also high, particularly among infants and small children, the number of deaths in these agrarian societies nearly equaled the number of births, so their populations did not grow rapidly. Then death rates began to fall in Europe and America. With birthrates remaining high, the result was far more births than deaths and therefore rapid growth in the number of people.

Some historians regard the European and American population boom as an important cause of subsequent industrialization; however, Asia also experienced growing population at that time but without similar effect, so these early linkages remain puzzling. Whether or not population growth was a cause of industrialization, industrialization surely contributed to population growth in the West, especially through improvements in the provision of food, clothing, shelter, and sanitation. Despite the horrible conditions that existed in some mines and factories at that time, and the appalling poverty of the lowest urban classes, life overall was healthier than in the grim environment of preindustrial Europe. In the "virgin" Americas, population growth during the eighteenth and nineteenth centuries was phenomenal as European-like settlements and technology swept across the vast lands taken from the Indians.

One might think that as the human population grew, people would space themselves out over the landscape, at least to the extent that food resources are spread out. In fact, the human tendency during periods of growth is to aggregate in fixed settlements, either transporting or manipulating the food supply so as to support these concentrations. This trend produced the towns and cities of the Agrarian/Urban Transformation. Although these were far greater concentrations of people than had existed before, most were barely "urban" by today's standards. Even Rome, probably the largest city of the ancient world, is estimated to have had a population of only 650,000 in AD 100; and as recently as 1800, less than 1 percent of the Earth's people lived in cities of 100,000 or more (Chandler and Fox, 1974). The trend toward concentration intensified as population growth accelerated. Industrial nations in Europe, America, and Japan, predominantly rural during the early nineteenth century, became predominantly urban in the twentieth century. As the population growth in Third World countries has exploded, especially since World War II, they, too, have concentrated in cities. In the year 2000, seven of the world's ten largest cities were in the Third World, and half of the Earth's people were urbanites.

Any growth in world population must be attributable to either an increase in births or a decrease in deaths, or both. We do not know which factor was most important for population growth during the Agrarian/Urban Transformation. Perhaps when people settled in stable communities their health improved and so the death rate fell, or perhaps their birthrate rose because of improved nutrition or because sedentary families space their children closer in time than do roving hunters and gatherers, but this is guesswork. We do know that recent growth—within the past 200 years—is the result of declining mortality, not rising fertility (with a few exceptions). It was not that people began to breed like rabbits; rather, they no longer died like flies (Weeks, 1986).

Changing Mortality

Everyone dies; the only uncertainties are when and how. In the year 2004, the oldest man in the United States died in my city, Syracuse N.Y., at the age of 112. Several American women are older. *Guinness World Records* (2004) tells of a French woman recently living to the age of 122. Today, people have a better chance of reaching 100 than ever before. But the great recent improvements in life expectancy have not come so much from extending old age as in protecting babies.

It has always been true that an "infant"—defined as a child in its first year of life—is considerably more likely to die than an older child or a young adult. After the first few years of life, the risk of death remains relatively low until sometime around middle age when it begins to increase, a pattern that still holds true in the United States. It is the reduction of the death rate at the beginning of life rather than during old age that has most improved life expectancy.

As recently as 1915, 10 percent of live births in America died in infancy, usually of infectious disease. Today, in most industrial countries the infant mortality rate is far less than 1 percent. Parents living in these nations fully expect all of their children to outlive them and probably to survive into old age. This remarkable improvement in the human condition, which came with industrialization, was initially due to rising living standards. People were better fed, better clothed, and better housed; drank cleaner water; and bathed more often—with soap (McKeown, 1976). Medical treatment played little part in this early gain. It was simply that people—especially children—were living healthier lives than before and therefore were less likely to die at an early age.

Not until the twentieth century did medicine contribute to improved life expectancy, first through vaccinations that protect against infectious disease. The first antibiotic drugs became available around the time of World War II, giving physicians a nearly miraculous weapon against bacterial (but not viral) diseases. The effects of these medical techniques on Americans is shown in Table 7.2, which compares major causes of deaths in

Table 7.2.   Death rates for selected causes in the United States, 1900 and 2004

Cause	1900	2004
Tuberculosis	17%	0%
Flu and pneumonia	17%	3%
Heart disease	14%	28%
Stroke	10%	7%
Accidents	8%	4%
Nephritis and nephrosis	8%	2%
Cancer	6%	23%
Infectious diseases of childhood	6%	0%
Other causes	14%	33%
	100%	100%

Sources: National Center for Health Statistics, *National Vital Statistics Reports* (Feb. 11, 2004); Bureau of the Census, *Historical Statistics of the United States, Colonial Times to 1957* (1960).

1900 and 2004. These changes are fairly typical of the industrial world during the twentieth century.

Tuberculosis, a bacterial infection of the lungs, was a leading cause of death in 1900, but it kills very few Americans today because it can be cured with antibiotic drugs, despite some drug-resistant strains. Flu (influenza), still a common disease, killed people by making them susceptible to pneumonia. More American soldiers died from the Great Flu Epidemic of 1918 than were killed in battle during World War I (Kolata, 1999). Nephritis and nephrosis, diseases of the kidney, also made their victims vulnerable to other lethal infections, all of which can now be controlled with antibiotics. Whooping cough (pertussis) killed more infants at the turn of the century than diphtheria, scarlet fever, and polio combined. Now, this gamut of childhood infections is of little concern, partly because of antibiotics but especially because of widespread preventive vaccinations that have largely eliminated these diseases. Today, polio and diphtheria rarely occur in the industrialized nations, although they still appear occasionally in the Third World.

With infectious disease declining as a cause of death, especially for young people, heart disease and cancer became the major killers of the second half of the twentieth century. Perhaps this is part of the reason for a currently popular but false myth that America is suffering from a rising cancer epidemic, usually blamed on increases in pollution and chemicals in the environment (Ames and Gold, 1989). Some of this apparent increase simply reflects improvements in diagnosis. For example, many breast and prostate cancers that once would have been overlooked are now discovered with more effective mammography and blood tests. (Apart from better diagnosis, there may be a real rise in breast cancer. On the other hand, stomach cancer has decreased.) But the main reason that cancer is found in a larger proportion of today's population than among their grandparents is that more people than ever before now survive to an age when cancer becomes a major problem. Despite tragic images that we may have of children stricken with the disease, cancer is mainly an affliction of the elderly. If we look at age-specific cancer rates, that is, the proportion of people of a given age who die of cancer, there has been little increase in most types of cancer since 1950 (Doll and Peto, 1981). The major exception is lung cancer, whose age-specific death rate has increased greatly during this century as a direct result of increased cigarette smoking since World War II.

Like cancer, heart attacks rarely strike people under the age of 50, and the emergence of heart disease as the major killer in the industrialized nations is also explained in part by our increased survivability to that age. However, there was also a real age-specific increase in heart disease, so that fifty-year-olds of the late twentieth century were more likely to have a heart attack than were fifty-year-olds in 1900. Cigarettes are again a culprit here, along with increased consumption of fatty foods and lack of physical exercise in sedentary jobs. Fortunately, the death rate from heart disease, while still high, is now receding in the United States, perhaps due to wide use of a class of drugs called "statins" and to better control of high blood pressure.

People in their teens and early twenties have rightly seen themselves as nearly invulnerable to fatal disease, although it is possible that AIDS will be an exception. That disease now takes a frightful toll in Sub-Saharan Africa, which suffers two-thirds of the world's HIV infections. In the United States and other industrialized nations, the few young people who die from other causes tend to be males and are usually victims of accidents (especially in automobiles) and less often of homicide (especially black males) and suicide; alcohol is often involved. There are times when warfare takes an appalling number of young men, but those are unusual circumstances.

Since World War II there have been rapid decreases in mortality rates (other than AIDS) in the Third World. Unlike the developed nations, where economically improved lifestyles initiated decreases in mortality, these poorer nations have benefited from medical and public health measures without necessarily showing improvements in their economic conditions. The result, of course, has been an explosion of population in the midst of poverty. This dismal situation should not blind us to the real accomplishment of improved health in the Third World. One truly remarkable achievement of the 1960s and 1970s was the total elimination of smallpox through a worldwide vaccination program coordinated by the World Health Organization. We have the technical means to make further improvements in Third World mortality (as well as in the poverty pockets of the developed countries). Working in the opposite direction, American and European tobacco companies are increasing sales of cigarettes in the Third World.

The Theory of Demographic Transition

For a century or more, the industrializing nations enjoyed decreasing death rates while their birthrates remained high, producing an unprecedented degree of population growth in the Northern Hemisphere. Not until the twentieth century did birthrates in the industrial countries began seriously falling (except for the "baby boom" years after World War II), reaching currently low levels of ten to twenty births per thousand per year. This is barely higher than current mortality rates in these nations of six to fifteen deaths per thousand per year. With yearly births again nearly equal to yearly deaths, population stopped growing. Today, population in the industrial world has stabilized and is even declining in places.

We can neatly summarize the demographic changes that most industrialized countries experienced within the past 200 years. Before industrialization, they had high birthrates and nearly as high death rates, so population growth was not very rapid. Then death rates fell, first because of economically improved lifestyles and later from improvements in public health and medicine. Since birthrates did not fall as quickly as death rates, populations soared. By the 1970s, birthrates in the industrialized countries had fallen, as if chasing after the plunging death rates. As a result, with births and deaths nearly equal, population began to level off. Figure 7.1 is a schematic illustration of this transition from low growth, to high growth, back to low growth.

This description of actual changes in the industrialized nations has been elaborated into a general theory of "demographic transition" that may apply to all nations. If the theory is correct,

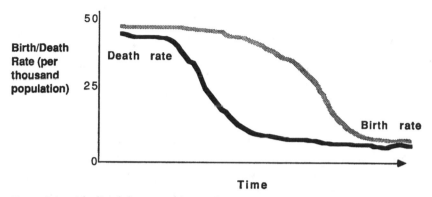

Figure 7.1. *Idealized demographic transition*

then the explosive population growth now being experienced by Third World nations ought to lessen as these nations modernize. This is a relatively optimistic view, suggesting that world population will stabilize more or less "automatically." Pessimists argue that the theory does not apply to the Third World and that population there will continue to grow unless heroic measures are taken to stop it. This controversial theory is important enough to examine why it might, or might not, apply to Third World nations.

At the beginning of the twentieth century, birth and death rates in the Third World were generally higher than were those in Europe on the eve of its industrialization, but this was perhaps the least crucial difference in these settings. Preindustrial Europe had a quickening commerce—fueled by the exploitation of colonies in Asia, Africa, and the New World—that was a precursor to its industrialization. The Third World is attempting to industrialize in a wholly different context, with many of its regions still dominated and exploited by former colonial powers. In general, Third World nations have not enjoyed the economically improved lifestyles that accompanied industrialization in Europe, America, and Japan. While their death rates have fallen, especially since World War II, this has been the result of improvements in public health and medicine, not of economic well-being. Perhaps this failure of economic development, so different from the historical transformation of the industrial countries, has put the demographic transition off track.

On the other hand, there have been changes across the Third World that encourage lower birth rates. As women increasingly work outside the home, become more educated, and move from farms to cities, they want fewer children. Indeed, birthrates in many Third World nations have started to fall, as the theory of demographic transition predicts. The critical remaining questions are whether they will fall in all regions of the world and fall far enough to extinguish growth. And if so, will this happen soon enough to keep world population within reasonable bounds?

Recent Changes in Population and Fertility

It is hard to know why a nation's birthrate changes from time to time because it is the aggregate of all the private decisions made by each family about how many children to have. Sometimes the husband and wife themselves do not fully understand their decisions, not to mention that babies often come without—or in spite of—intentional decision making.

The availability of modern methods of contraception—birth control pills, intrauterine devices (IUDs), condoms, diaphragms, foam, sterilization, and so on—makes family planning simpler, and this is an important element in population control. But there were always techniques available for limiting the number of children conceived. Among the most important historically were delayed marriages, periods within marriage of sexual abstinence, prolonged breast-feeding (decreasing the likelihood of impregnation), avoiding intercourse during the fertile phase of the menstrual cycle, abortion, and infanticide. Thus, the high birthrates of agrarian societies do not reflect an inability to control reproduction as much as a disinclination to do so. Why do agrarian people want so many children?

Until recently, an unavoidable fact of family life was the high probability—perhaps one chance in four—that a newborn would die before it reached adulthood. Parents who limited themselves to two children took a serious chance that neither would grow up to care for them in old age. If they wanted a surviving male child, either because men had more earning power or were more valued in the society, then the chance of success was half that. Only by having many children could parents be confident that some would outlive them.

Also, there are purely economic reasons for farmers or herdsmen to have many children, for they are a major source of labor in the fields, in tending livestock, and in household chores—including care for younger siblings. Agrarian community norms often encourage large families, especially many sons, because young men add to a settlement's fighting power as well as to its economic and social prominence. Often, parents are encouraged by their own parents to have more children, for these additions strengthen the household. Since the status of women is typically subservient to men in agrarian societies, a woman's value is often measured by her ability to bear children, especially sons. Taken together, there is a strong incentive to breed (Caldwell and Caldwell, 1990).

As new economic opportunities emerge during the transition to industrialism, many of these incentives for large families diminish and even reverse. Whereas children are productive workers on a family farm or in a village economy based on the old barter system, they contribute little to cash economies where the family is supported by wage earners. Now young children become an economic liability, especially if they demand their mother's time when she too could be earning money outside the home.

Children may eventually get jobs of their own and contribute wages to the family, but parents in an industrial economy understand that one's earning capacity is enhanced by job training and general education, so they often encourage children to go to school, expecting them to get higher paying jobs later. Education is costly, not only in tuition but in supporting the nonearning student until he or she is ready to find paying jobs. Still, many parents regard this as a good investment if economic opportunities are available for their newly educated children, and so they will pay the price, at least as much as they can afford. But it simply costs too much to educate fully a lot of kids. Therefore, many parents make an explicit tradeoff: rather than bearing many children and investing a little in each one, they bear only a few and invest heavily in all of them to ensure their upward mobility. This was precisely the reasoning of European and Asian immigrants to the United States at the turn of the twentieth century when families commonly had five or six children. Many of these "second-generation" children opted for smaller families and then supported their children as far as they could through the accessible American school system, preparing them to take advantage of good job opportunities.

These changes, so close to the experiences of many of our own families, are easy to understand in an improving economy. But what about those Third World countries today where conditions are not so rosy? Can we expect a similar decline in birthrates?

To some extent we can. Changes that are occurring even in the absence of economic improvement still work against large families, if not with the full force provided by the betterment of lifestyles. The movement of rural populations to teeming cities, even if it does not improve a family's lot, places a premium on its living space. Many children, easily accommodated in open country communities, become an increased burden in crowded urban housing. More important is the transformation of women's roles from peasant homemakers to urban wage earners, so that wives in the cities cannot devote as much of their resources to childrearing as their rural mothers did. Also, women who move to cities are removed from the traditional expectations of their communities and extended families to produce as many children as they can. With the spread of easy forms of contraception, these women can take more initiative in controlling their reproduction.

The simple fact that nearly every newborn now survives— once parents come to believe that—removes some of the incentive to bear many children as a way of ensuring that a few will reach adulthood. Also, it is possible that parents form stronger emotional attachments to infants whom they can depend upon surviving than to those whom they know might die in the first year. Anecdotes about the doting of today's Japanese and Chinese parents (and grandparents) on their children, even exceeding the parental indulgence of children in the West, suggest that increased attachment to children accompanies their increased survivability (Baum, 1987).

It is worth emphasizing the uncertainty in our understanding of declining fertility and to warn against overoptimism that all birthrates in the Third World will "automatically" fall far enough and fast enough. China is one nation that found these natural processes inadequate and in 1979 introduced a policy of one child per family, no doubt the most ambitious family planning program in the world. A couple pledging to have only one child received a monthly allowance for childrearing, and if they were city dwellers they got special access to new housing. An "only child" got preferential school admission and later, special access to jobs. Women who became pregnant in violation of the policy might encounter strong social pressure to terminate the pregnancy. Couples who had too many children were subject to monetary fines. If such compulsion is difficult to reconcile with Western liberal values, it is no more compatible with the traditional Chinese emphasis on large, extended families.

Whether because of its one-child policy or, more likely, the remarkable improvement in China's economy, that nation has successfully reduced its birthrate. Column 3 of table 7.1 shows that in 1970–1975, the average Chinese woman gave birth to 4.9 babies. By 2000–2005, that number was down to 1.8—below the replacement level. (Still, China's population will continue to grow as long as there is a disproportionate number of young females who have not yet completed their families.) In 2004, China reported a yearly population increase of only 0.6 percent—a very low rate for a Third World nation (column 2). With its population near 1.3 billion, that is still a net increase of 8 million Chinese per year.

While no other region of the Third World has brought fertility and population growth down to the levels China has achieved, nearly all regions have made progress in that direction. Between the periods 1970–1975 and 2000–2005, Latin America reduced average fertility from 5.1 babies per woman to 2.4. Over the same years, Middle East fertility dropped from 6.2 to

3.0; Southeast Asia dropped from 5.7 to 2.6; and South Asia dropped from 5.6 to 3.3. Thus, most regions of the Third World cut fertility in half during the last quarter of the twentieth century, and this downward trend continues.

The exception is Sub-Saharan Africa, that region of greatest misery. Here, there has been only small progress, with fertility barely dropping from 6.8 babies per woman to 5.4. Very large families are still the norm in Africa, and population continues its rapid growth.

Age-Sex Structure

The average (median) age of people living in the Third World is roughly eighteen-years-old, much younger than the about thirty-five-year-old average for people in the industrialized countries. This difference is not so much due to shorter life expectancies in the Third World as to greater birthrates.

To see this, it is useful to illustrate a population's age-sex structure with a pyramid like the one at the left in figure 7.2, which is typical of a Third World nation. Its total population is divided into males and females and then into five-year age categories. Horizontal bars, running from the central vertical line to the left, show the percentages of the total population who are males in each age category. Bars running to the right show percentages of females in each age. The age categories increase from the bottom to the top of the diagram. The term "pyramid" comes from the fact that historically there were more young than old people, and thus the younger (lower) bars were longer than the older (upper) ones (Yaukey, 1985).

In 1900, the age-sex structure of the industrialized nations looked much like this left pyramid, but by 1980 it had changed into the shape at the right in figure 7.2. Why? First, childhood mortality dropped to the extent that nearly everyone lived through their childbearing years. Thus, as the youngsters in each five-year category aged, nearly all of them survived to move into the next older category, so there was no longer an automatic shrinkage by death as one moved up the pyramid. Sec-

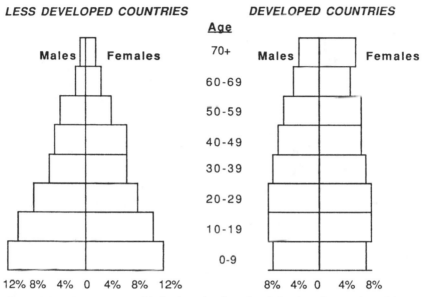

Figure 7.2.   Age-sex pyramids for less developed and developed countries, 1985

ond, and more crucial, was that the fertility rate fell to about two babies per woman. As a result, the number of children born in each five-year period roughly equaled the number in their parents' period. In other words, by bringing the fertility rate down to the replacement level, the number of people in each age category became constant (at least until the advanced ages when most people die). Therefore, the pyramid changed into a column.

Now it should be clear why average age is much lower in the Third World than in the industrialized countries. The Third World's population is bunched into the lowest-age categories. Thus, the median person is a teenager. Industrialized populations are spread fairly evenly by age. Thus, median age is in the middle years, about the mid-30s. Many people find it counterintuitive to learn that this difference is due to falling birthrates, not to improving life expectancies. It may help to recognize that any industrial society can return to a pyramidal shape simply by increasing its birthrate so that each new five-year age category has more infants than the prior one.

A comparison of the age-sex structures in figure 7.2 shows further that the ratio of males to females is lower in the developed than in the less developed regions of the world. In all societies, about 105 boy babies are born for every 100 girls. But this excess of males eventually disappears because males have a higher death rate than females at all ages except perhaps when women face the hazards of childbirth. In the industrialized countries, the reduction of death rates favors women, making childbirth safer and helping in later years too. At higher ages, women outnumber men more and more. In industrialized nations, the elderly are predominately women.

A society with a high proportion of children must devote its attention and resources to child care and schooling. Street crime and crimes of violence are overwhelmingly committed by males in their teens and early twenties (Wilson and Herrnstein, 1985), and pregnancies—whether planned or unplanned—occur most often in females of these ages. All of these problems increase or decrease, depending upon whether the number of young people is increasing or decreasing (relative to the number of older people). New jobs must be provided as more people enter the workforce, or there will be an increase in unemployment and its attendant problems. As more people start new families, there is pressure on the supply of housing. As people age, retire, and enter the years of increasing death rates, there is more demand for health care and maintenance of the elderly.

Important differences in the problems of the more and less developed regions of the world stem directly from their differing age-sex structures. The Third World, with about 40 percent of its population under fifteen years, has overwhelming problems of caring for these young people, eventually providing them jobs, and controlling high levels of crime and pregnancy. The industrialized world has the opposite problem of a large and growing elderly population that must be sustained. Conflicts between industrial and less developed societies necessarily pit an older population against a younger one. Israelis, for example, have a median age in the mid-thirties, while the median Palestinian is a teenager. The old and young see things differently and behave differently.

Urbanization

A preoccupation with the size of the world population may blind one to the problems caused by its concentration into huge and densely settled cities, their sprawling slums barely touched by urban services. Only two urban agglomerations, New York and Tokyo, held more than 10 million people in 1950; by 1985, nine cities were that large; in 2000, eighteen cities exceeded 10 million inhabitants. By 2003, according to UN statisticians, 48 percent of the world's population lived in urban areas; by 2007, the world will have more urban residents than rural residents. Even with a drastic slowing of global population growth, cities will continue to grow, becoming increasingly unmanageable.

Since today's urban areas have usually spread far beyond their original municipal boundaries, the terms "city" or "urban agglomeration" mean not only the municipality itself but also the urban areas connected to it. For example, the "New York" urban agglomeration, as defined by the UN (2004), contains not only New York City but also Newark and White Plains; "Los Angeles" includes Long Beach and Anaheim. These boundaries are to some extent arbitrary, so population counts depend on how an urban area is defined.

Table 7.3. Population (in millions) of the world's ten largest cities in 1950, 1975, and 2000

1950		1975		2000	
New York	12.3	Tokyo	26.6	Tokyo	34.5
Tokyo	11.3	New York	15.9	Mexico City	18.1
London	8.4	Shanghai	11.4	New York	17.8
Paris	5.4	Mexico City	10.7	Sao Paulo	17.1
Moscow	5.4	Osaka	9.8	Mumbai (Bombay)	16.1
Shanghai	5.3	Sao Paulo	9.6	Calcutta	13.1
Rhein/Ruhr	5.3	Buenos Aires	9.1	Shanghai	12.9
Buenos Aires	5.0	Los Angeles	8.9	Buenos Aires	12.6
Chicago	5.0	Paris	8.6	Delhi	12.4
Calcutta	4.5	Beijing	8.6	Los Angeles	11.8

Source: UN (2004)

Since the beginning of industrialization, growing cities have been a hallmark of the developed countries. In 1950, seven of the world's ten largest urban areas were located in industrialized nations. Since then, as population growth leveled off in the industrialized nations but exploded in the Third World, the most rapidly growing cities are in the less developed nations. By 2000, only three of the ten largest (Tokyo, New York, and Los Angeles) were in industrialized nations. *Almost all of the growth of the world's total population between 2000 and 2030 is expected to be absorbed by the urban areas of the Third World.*

Birthrates in cities are usually lower than in the countryside. Why then are Third World cities growing so much faster than total Third World population? The reason is that rural people are migrating to the cities, seeking a better life. Younger people especially see little future for themselves in the countryside. Migrants in nearly every Third World country are attracted to its cities, crowding its housing, transportation, and schools; taxing its medical and social services; and overwhelming its water, sewage, and electrical facilities.

Mexico City, by UN count the second largest urban area in the world, is a salient example. Once the center of Aztec culture, it was larger than any city in Europe when Cortes destroyed it in 1521. If the site was a practical one then, it is not today. Water must be pumped over the surrounding mountains to reach the city, while waste is pumped out. Situated on a mile-high lake bed, Mexico City is sinking into its porous soil, in some places ten inches per year. Near the middle of the city, the famous Angel statue, built on pilings set deep into solid ground, holds its place while buildings and streets around it sink, so that each year the Angel seems to ascend further into the smoggy sky (McDowell, 1984).

Mexico City receives a tremendous inflow of rural immigrants. It is where the jobs are, holding one-third of the nation's factory and commercial positions and two-thirds of the national bureaucracy. Work in the city, when it is available, pays many times what one can earn in the countryside. But jobs are not the city's only attraction; it is a lively and exciting place with broad boulevards and gleaming office buildings, splendid churches, beautiful fountains and flower beds, high culture and popular entertainment, spectacular museums, and a major university. The city offers the opportunity for a modern lifestyle that cannot be attained in the rural areas.

With half of Mexico City's population under the age of sixteen, there are plenty of young mothers to increase the population, even with a now-lowered birthrate. Priests in this Catholic country condone contraception but not abortion, and family planning efforts have been very successful by the standards of the Third World. Still, there are too many people.

Perhaps 30 percent of Mexico City's families sleep in a single room. Half live in housing that fails to meet building codes or without legal title to the site. In many areas of the city, newcomers have set up their own shanties. Mexican authorities have tried to prevent squatters from building these shacks in a futile effort to limit the city's growth and hold control of its land. A common response by the squatters is to band together in secret, planning an "invasion" of unoccupied land near the city. Then, in one night, they occupy the land, quickly raising their shanties on prearranged sites before police can evict them. Once established, the squatters are hard to dislodge. As their fortunes improve, they convert their shacks into permanent houses, adding second stories and bringing in utilities, and even establishing quasi-legal rights to their homesites. Such squatter invasions occur in many countries, and the shantytowns often turn into stable neighborhoods, much better places to live than the central city's slums (Mangin, 1967).

Crowded shantytowns, inadequate construction, and corrupt administration all make the city vulnerable to natural or man-made disaster. In 1984, a massive explosion of gas storage tanks in Mexico City killed hundreds of people living in squatter settlements that had grown up around the facility. Since there is no record of who was living in these hovels, and many victims were burned to ash, authorities could only guess at the number dead. The city had a major earthquake in 1985 that killed more than 4,000 people primarily because high-rise apartment buildings were constructed so poorly that they collapsed on their inhabitants.

City services never keep up with the increasing population. In Mexico City, large portions of the population have no running water or sewage facilities. Much of the city's garbage is unprocessed, and the rest feeds legions of rats. A combination of chemical and biological poisons kills an estimated 30,000 children per year through respiratory and gastrointestinal diseases (Friedrich, Chavira, and DeVoss, 1984).

Mexico City opened a modern subway in 1969, which, by 1985, crammed in 4 million commuters daily. Men are restricted to separate cars from women and children because of the crush. The city contains nearly half the nation's motor vehicles, producing the worst smog and one of the highest accident rates in the world. These are some of the reasons why one of the city's planners calls Mexico City a "case study in urban disaster," and another says of it, "At the least we can be a huge warning to the world" (McDowell, 1984).

The industrialized countries have urban problems, too, although not as dire as the Third World. The depressed central cities of the United States, with their impoverished and crime-ridden slums, are the clearest example of troubles that can be caused by a heavy concentration of population, even when the nation's total population is nearly stable and there is abundant land, food, and other resources for the number of people.

Are Fewer Better?

By any reasonable standard, many developing countries already have too many people and continue to grow too fast. For these nations, and for those who would aid them, population control is a top priority (Brown and Jacobson, 1986). Further slowing of birthrates in the Third World would not only stabilize total population but would also relieve pressure on the cities by reducing the number of migrants from the countryside. Reduced birthrates would narrow the age-sex pyramid, causing the average age in the Third World to rise, thus increasing the proportion of productive people in the work force while diminishing the high percentage of dependent children.

However, in the industrialized world, where populations are already stable or dropping, further limits would serve little purpose. Indeed, limits might actually be harmful by reducing the productive workforce needed to support growing numbers of dependent elderly people in these nations.

The simple "Malthusian" view of global population outlined at the beginning of this chapter, which teaches that all growth must be stopped, is based on the assumption that the total number of people is the essential problem. This view gained its modern currency in the 1960s (Ehrlich, 1968), a time when populations around the world were accelerating furiously. Prior to the year 1650, when humans numbered roughly 500 million, it took on average about 1,500 years for the size of the population to double. The next doubling, from 500 million to a billion, occurred by 1850, only 200 years later. It took just another 80 years to reach 2 billion in 1930, and then only 45 years to double again to 4 billion (Ehrlich and Ehrlich, 1970). This rapidly accelerating growth was often illustrated by showing population shooting upward like a rocket with no end in sight. It was not obvious in the 1960s that the baby boom had ended, so some observers feared that the industrialized nations were growing rapidly too. At that time, one often heard such projections as: at current growth rates, it will take only 600 years for there to be one person per square meter of ice-free land!

With the advantage of hindsight, it is now clear that the industrialized world's short-lived baby boom ended in the 1960s and that marked population growth is now limited to the Third World, particularly its cities. In most of the Third World, fertility and the rate of population increase are rapidly diminishing, most successfully in China and Latin America. There have also been improvements in the Middle East, Southeast Asia, and South Asia, but in these regions fertility and the rate of population growth remain fairly high. As usual, Sub-Saharan Africa presents the most depressing picture. With slight reductions in fertility, the average woman continues to have 5.4 babies in her lifetime. This natural increase is partly countered by the AIDS death toll, but still population grows 2 percent yearly, a rate that if continued will cause a doubling of the African population in thirty-five years.

Assuming more improvement in Africa, it seems likely that world population will level off in this century, the outstanding questions being when and at what number? UN statisticians in 2003 projected a world population of 8.9 billion for the year 2050, still growing slightly. (Considering uncertainties, the statisticians also offered a "low" projection for 2050 of 7.4 billion, already past peak, and a "high" projection of 10.6 billion, still increasing). The United Nations suggested that a peak population of 9.2 billion would be reached in about 2075, with some decline afterward.

We cannot say if the median UN estimate, a less-than-doubling of population in about seventy years, would be more or less tolerable than the doubling we have already experienced in the past forty years. Surely a leveling off at 7 or 8 billion would be better. But in either case, the total number may not be as crucial as its distribution, concentration, and the rapidity with which we reach it. These importantly affect our ability to accommodate to growth.

Even if the number of people in the Third World stabilized very soon, Third World cities will continue to grow rapidly, fed by migration from the countryside. Presently, the smaller cities, under 500,000 population, are growing most quickly, giving some relief to the largest urban agglomerates (UN, 2004).

With some industrialized nations fretting about their declining populations and insufficient workforce, there is some logic to easing immigration from the poorer to the richer nations. This is already plentiful, if often illegal, for example the flow of impoverished Latin Americans who are eager to work at low-wage jobs in the United States, which seems beneficial to people on both sides of the border.

No matter what the number of people in the world, whether more or less than we have now, it is exceedingly difficult to provide all of them with an adequate lifestyle. This is probably occurring better now than in 1960 when world population was only half that of 2000. To continue this improvement will require increases in production without at the same time depleting scarce materials and poisoning the Earth.

Perhaps the greatest impediment to this goal is not the growing number of people in the Third World but the enormous and often wasteful per capita consumption of resources in the affluent societies. The average American consumes more energy than 10 Colombians or 100 Sudanese. One remaining argument for limiting the populations of the industrial societies is that each additional industrial person consumes much more than his or her share of nonrenewable resources and accounts for a similarly disproportionate share of environmental pollution. True enough, but it does not follow that a reduction of the American population by, say, 10 percent would reduce resource consumption by that much.

Many of our resource expenditures are for large systems like interstate highways, ports, and military forces, which would not change much if the population declined. In any case, why attack that problem indirectly by reducing the number of people? It would be more efficient to strive directly for reductions in wasteful consumption and pollution. These are issues for the next chapter.

8

Technology, Resources, and Environment

"We are running out of oil, we are running out of oil," cried Chicken Little. "And if we use it all up the sky will fall!" Indeed, we are using up our petroleum, but if the sky falls, it will not be because the oil is all gone.

Oil is a good example of the minerals that industries around the world drill for or dig from the ground to use as fuels or raw materials. Most of these are finite resources, meaning that what is now in the ground is all there is. Pumping oil from the Earth, like sipping soda from a glass, will empty the container, and soon we will find ourselves thirstily slurping up the last drop. Right? Wrong!

Oil, like most finite resources, is distributed throughout the globe in many different ways. Lots of it sits in pools around the Persian Gulf, where all one need do is drill a shallow hole in the ground and let it gush to the surface. In other places, it is deeper, under hard rock, and drilling is difficult. Canada has huge deposits of petroleum in its Athabasca tar sands, mixed as a gritty ooze with other material from which it can be separated, but this is a messy task that leaves behind a noxious residue of dirty sand. A vast amount of oil is mixed in shale rock in the American Rocky Mountains; one can actually smash the shale with a hammer and squeeze oil out of it. But crushing this rock on a large scale would require extensive mining of parts of the scenic Rockies, leaving behind huge amounts of crushed rock. Coal is a hydrocarbon, like petroleum, and can be chemically converted to oil, but this too is costly, requires mining a lot of coal, and produces large amounts of unwanted residue.

If we include all of these sources in our inventory, there is a vast amount of oil available, but most of it is more costly and troublesome to obtain than what is in the shallow pools of the Persian Gulf. It is the cheap and easily available oil that is scarce, not all oil. As the easy oil runs out, people will still be able to get more if they want it badly enough to pay the costs of obtaining it (Yergin, 1991; Roberts, 2004).

We will speak of three kinds of costs that must be paid for hard-to-reach resources. First is monetary expense. As the resources in demand become scarcer, their prices rise, a simple consequence of the economic law of supply and demand. It then becomes worthwhile for resource producers to spend more money themselves in extracting the resources from the Earth and in developing improved technology to help them do this. A second kind of cost is pollution, which we use here as a general term referring to all forms of environmental degradation that inevitably accompany the extraction and consumption of resources, including mine holes, production of noxious waste, and the physical and aesthetic deterioration of ground, air, and water quality. The third kind of cost is increased risk to health, both to production workers who may experience greater hazards in extracting the hard-to-reach resources and to the public at large whose increased risk comes from increases in pollution, accidents, and other dangerous exposures.

These three factors—monetary expense, environmental pollution, and health risk—will usually increase as we seek ever harder-to-reach deposits of any resource, although periodically a new technology will lessen their impacts. Still, these costs will eventually become so high that we will reduce and finally give up our use of that resource, long before we literally run out of it. (Higher prices also impel resource users to seek cheaper substitutes, which may depress the demand and therefore the price of the resource originally sought.) Expense, pollution, and health risk are far bigger practical barriers to our unlimited use of oil than the simple fact that there is a finite amount of it in the Earth. If the sky falls, as Chicken Little fears, it will not be because the oil is gone but because we paid too high a price for it.

Instead of picturing the Earth as a soda glass filled with oil that can be drained dry, a better image is the Earth as an oil-soaked sponge. At first we can squeeze oil out easily, but soon we must squeeze harder, and eventually it takes so much strength to get a little oil that we stop trying although we have not emptied the sponge. The increasing muscular effort, the filth on our hands from squeezing, and the wear and tear on the sponge, which prevent it from springing back to its original shape, are all analogous to the costs of extraction borne by people and the Earth.

Are Renewables Better Than Finite Resources?

We will examine energy production from finite and renewable sources to illustrate the interplay between resource exploitation and costs. What we learn about fuels will apply as well to other kinds of resources, including minerals, land, vegetation, water, and the air.

Renewable Energy Sources

Since the oil shortages of the 1970s, there has been renewed interest in renewable energy sources like solar, hydropower (from waterfalls), windmills, and wood or other "biomass" crops that can be burned for fuel. These sources are not limited in ultimate quantity; when they are used, they are not used up. Solar energy is continuously replenished as long as the sun shines; wood and other biomass crops can be regrown within years. You cannot use up the wind or the flow of water since these are eternally in motion around the Earth.

In energy consumption, as in other mineral uses, shifting our reliance from finite to renewable materials is especially attractive if one accepts the soda glass image of finite resources, since the great appeal of the renewables is that they will never drain the glass dry. This argument is less compelling to those of us who regard the sponge image as truer, for we do not believe that the Earth can actually be drained of its finite contents. The costs of "sucking on the straw"—in terms of money, pollution, and health—will become prohibitive; and we will choke ourselves long before the world's supplies of coal, oil, and natural gas are depleted. Therefore, that particular difference between renewable and finite sources—that one will run out but not the other—is not very relevant.

The more crucial question is: which energy sources cost more to use during a particular historical period, the renewables or the finite fuels? If a renewable source of energy kills more people, costs more money, and is more polluting than a finite energy source, there would be little to recommend its use.

For example, during the energy shortages of the 1970s, some advocates of renewables encouraged wood burning for home heating in preference to fossil fuels or nuclear energy, as in the slogan, "Split wood, not atoms." Wood stoves became popular in parts of the United States, but after the first wave of enthusiasm, and as oil prices came down, many people found wood burning a costly and inconvenient method of heating their homes. The incomplete combustion of most home stoves produced noxious air pollution, including carcinogenic substances. Deaths from fires caused by wood stoves—often through faulty installation—were distressingly frequent, averaging 130 killed per year from 1980 to 1987 (U.S. Home Heating, 1989). Also, despite being renewable in principle, wood became scarce and expensive in many locales. Today, there is less enthusiasm for wood stoves as a replacement for finite fuels.

Every energy source, whether renewable or finite, has both advantages and disadvantages. Fuels that exist on the Earth in a limited quantity ought not to be disqualified from use by that fact alone. In comparing the desirability of different energy paths, one must consider the trade-offs between cost and advantage among the various options. Historically, finite fuels have provided benefits that were not available from renewable sources, and they may continue to do so.

Fossil Fuels

The common power sources of agrarian society were all renewable. Only with the coming of industrialization were they largely replaced by the finite "fossil fuels"—coal, oil, and natural gas—formed from the remains of plants and animals that lived millions of years ago and were buried under pressure in the Earth. When the Industrial Revolution began in Britain in the eighteenth century, cotton mills were powered by waterwheels pushed by rushing streams, and homes were heated by burning wood. Coal, which had been little used as a fuel, became an inexpensive substitute for heating homes as wood became scarce and expensive. With the development of the coal-fired steam engine, coal became the prime energy source for factories and then for railroad locomotives. Not only did coal have the advantage of relative abundance, but it also contains much more energy per pound than does wood, making it easier to transport and store. Coal has disadvantages, as the British knew well because the air of their industrial towns became filthy with soot. But they accepted the trade-off of dirty air and its attendant ills for the cheap and concentrated energy provided by coal. Of course, the plant owners did not live in the dirtiest parts of town, and the workers who did had little voice in the matter

Oil is another finite fossil fuel, chemically similar to coal (except that oil contains more hydrogen) and formed in nearly the same way, but it has the great advantage of being liquid. Its use grew greatly during this century, along with that of automobiles powered by internal combustion engines, which require a fuel that flows and is easily vaporized. The United States has gone to war to protect oil supplies in the Middle East because, at present, oil is the most practical fuel with which to run a nation of cars, trucks, and airplanes. Eventually, it may be replaced with renewable liquid fuels like alcohol, which can be distilled from fermented corn, beets, or other crops. But there are always trade-offs. For one, energy in the forms of fertilizer and farming machinery must be used to grow the corn that will be converted to alcohol, so the net amount of energy gained in the whole process is not very high. Also, if the entire U.S. corn crop were devoted to alcohol production, it would fuel less than one fourth of the nation's cars (Flavin and Pollock, 1985).

All fuels that burn in air—whether finite or renewable—are compounds made of hydrogen and carbon and are therefore called "hydrocarbons." Burning (or oxidation) is simply the chemical combination of a hydrocarbon fuel with oxygen, producing carbon dioxide (CO_2), water (H_2O), and heat. The water that is formed in combustion is no problem. If the burnt fuel is wood or another biomass crop that is replenished, then the growing vegetation will absorb from the atmosphere as much CO_2 as was liberated during burning. However, CO_2 added to the atmosphere by burning fossil fuels cannot be easily withdrawn and therefore is a major contributor to the gradual warming of the Earth's atmosphere; this is called the "greenhouse effect."

Sunlight easily passes through the transparent glass roof of a greenhouse. When it strikes the opaque ground or a plant, the sunbeam gives up energy in the form of heat. Then the beam reflects back from the ground or plant and "tries" to pass through the glass again, but being less energetic (since it has given up heat), it cannot do this as easily as before, so the beam remains "trapped" in the greenhouse, reflecting back and forth and giving up more energy, which heats the interior further. This is one reason why a greenhouse, or a closed car, gets very hot in the sunlight.

By adding CO_2 and certain other gases to the atmosphere, the transparency of the air becomes more glasslike, allowing energetic sunlight to enter but becoming more opaque to reflected sunbeams that have given up some of their energy. The result is the gradual heating of the atmosphere, as if the Earth were a giant greenhouse. This process is well understood, and there is no serious doubt that humans are presently warming the atmosphere by our fuel consumption, although scientists disagree on the precise extent of warming. Heating the atmosphere only a few degrees will have important effects on climate, including melting polar ice, raising sea levels, and flooding coastal areas. Regions that are now cold may become warm and hospitable. Presently good farming regions may become arid. No one knows the extent to which such changes will be harmful or beneficial, but clearly they are serious consequences of our enormous use of fossil fuels.

Coal and oil contain sulfur as an impurity, and during burning this reacts with oxygen to form sulfuric acid (H_2SO_4), a major component of acid rain, and sulfur dioxide (SO_2), which is believed to cause much of the damage to health from polluted air or smog. Natural gas (not to be confused with gasoline), the third major fossil fuel, is mostly methane, a simple molecule that contains nothing but hydrogen and carbon and therefore burns cleanly, adding no sulfur to the environment. As a bonus, methane burns very efficiently, too, producing only two-thirds or less CO_2 than the oil or coal needed to obtain the same amount of energy (Gibbons et al., 1989) and thus contributing less to the greenhouse effect. However, when any hydrocarbon, methane included, is burned some oxygen combines with nitrogen in the air, forming nitric acid—another component of acid rain—and other nitrogen compounds that pollute the air. Ozone (O_3) is another harmful component of smog, produced when sunlight acts on unburned hydrocarbons emitted in vehicle exhaust.

Natural gas is found with oil. Natural gas was once regarded as a nuisance because it was difficult to transport and so was burned off at the wellhead. Now that industry has learned to send natural gas through pipelines, it is regarded as the most valuable fossil fuel for heating. One of its important disadvantages, beyond those of any hydrocarbon, is that gas leaks can explode with great force, doing much damage to buildings and people. Considering how much natural gas is used today and how explosive it is, the technology for handling this fuel has been remarkably safe.

Another disadvantage of gas is that easily available supplies may be strained within decades. What then? There are several options, depending on how badly people want methane. A lot of natural gas exists in deep, unexploited deposits in the earth; these will be costlier to tap, but that could be done if people are willing to pay for it (Burnett and Ban, 1989). Another option is to make gas from coal, as was done commercially during the "gaslight era" of the early twentieth century. Or, like alcohol, it can be fermented from vegetation. One proposal, not wholly frivolous, notes that animals produce methane in their intestinal tracts as a by-product of the digestive process and then expel it as waste. By collecting the flatus of all the cattle in the country, one could accumulate an impressive amount of methane. Of course, there are trade-offs to consider.

We are now seeing increased use of liquefied natural gas (LNG). LNG is simply natural gas cooled to a sufficiently low temperature that it liquefies and is therefore transportable on large refrigerated ships, bringing supplies from across the oceans. On arrival at an American terminal, LNG tanks are off-loaded, and the material is allowed to warm and evaporate for normal use. A difficulty with LNG transport is the potential for an accident or a terrorist attack that would breach the refrigerated tanks, allowing a methane cloud to spread over a seaport. Any spark could produce a devastating explosion with much loss of life.

Trade-offs

The simple truism to remember when evaluating the desirability of any resource use is that there is no free lunch! Every option has its difficulties, and one must always consider the trade-off of costs for benefits.

Table 8.1 summarizes the major advantages and disadvantages of eight important energy sources. It is tempting to skim over such intricacies, but these details are worthwhile for they show how a case can be made for or against the use of each option, since each source has its particular pros and cons.

Even such clean, renewable sources as solar and wind power have disadvantages, most obviously that they are intermittent, working only when the sun shines or the wind blows. Other problems stem from the low "energy density" of these sources. Unlike coal or oil, which pack a lot of energy in a small amount of fuel, the power in sunlight and wind power is diffuse, or spread out; the sun that shines on one square yard, or the wind that blows through it, carries only a little bit of power. Therefore,

Table 8.1. Major advantages and disadvantages of important energy sources

Advantages	Disadvantages
COAL (finite)	
Plentiful supply of easy-to-reach deposits, inexpensive, high energy content per pound of fuel.	Burning causes air pollution, global warming, and large amount of ash; mining is hazardous to miners and disfigures the earth; coal is dirty and bulky to transport and store.
OIL (finite)	
Flows, easy to transport, vaporizes, high energy content per pound of fuel.	Easy-to-reach deposits limited and vulnerable to foreign interference, refineries are polluting, accidental spills during transport, burning causes air pollution and global warming, sometimes expensive, has been a cause of war.
NATURAL GAS (finite)	
Clean burning, easy to ship by pipeline, relatively inexpensive, high energy content per pound.	Easy-to-reach deposits are limited, contributes to global warming though less than other fossil fuels, can explode, LNG could cause catastrophic accidents.
NUCLEAR POWER	
Fuel has very high energy content; plentiful; easy to mine, process, and transport; no air pollution or global warming.	Radiation must be controlled, possibility of catastrophic accidents, radioactive waste is very long lived, expensive, weapons proliferation, public opposition.
HYDRO (renewable)	
No air pollution or greenhouse effect, often cheap.	Requires damming of rivers, good sites are limited, possibility of catastrophic accidents, silting.
PHOTOVOLTAIC (renewable)	
Free and inexhaustible sunlight is converted directly to electricity without requiring a turbine, no air pollution or global warming.	Expensive at present, low energy density of sunlight requires a very large area of collectors, does not work at night.

(continued)

Table 8.1. (*continued*)

Advantages	Disadvantages
WIND (renewable)	
Free and inexhaustible wind produces no air pollution or global warming.	Expensive at present; low energy density of wind requires a very large array of windmills, only works when the wind blows, birds fly into windmills.
WOOD/BIOMASS (renewable)	
Fuel can be grown easily and is inexpensive when plentiful, home fireplaces are aesthetically pleasing.	Low energy content per pound, bulky to transport and store, burning causes air pollution, logging is hazardous, faulty wood stoves are fire hazards.

numerous solar collectors or windmills—each collecting a small amount of energy—must be manufactured and installed across large areas of land or sea in order to collect as much energy as is concentrated in a single fuel-burning power plant. It would take roughly forty square miles of solar collectors or windmills, the exact amount depending on their efficiency and the conditions of sunlight, to generate as much electricity as one large nuclear or fossil-fuel power plant of 1,000-megawatt capacity (Dominici, 2004). Many people object to placing windmills across the countryside or near coastlines to utilize brisk sea breezes. Furthermore, the nonrenewable materials needed to build so many collectors have appreciable costs (Whipple, 1980). Even renewable sun and wind power are not free.

Estimating Health Risks

Assume that there are two technologies, A and B, both capable of generating a given amount of energy. We would like to implement the least costly option. It is easy in principle to compare their monetary costs; one simply tallies the number of dollars required to reach the goal by technology A, makes a similar calculation for technology B, and sees which option is cheapest. For example, in 2004, despite rapidly falling costs for solar energy, the price of electricity generated from photovoltaic cells at a residential installation in a sunny climate was roughly 30-40 cents per kilowatt-hour, about eight or nine times the price of electricity generated by conventional fossil fuel or nuclear power plants (Dominici, 2004).

It is harder to compare the environmental costs of two technologies if A would dirty the air and B would foul the water. Here, there is no common unit like a dollar that can be used to measure the two kinds of damage, so any evaluation of these options in environmental terms is necessarily more subjective than when we weigh their dollar costs. In terms of environmental aesthetics, nearly everyone prefers sunshine to coal as an energy source; but most choices of this kind, say, between solar and natural gas, are more ambiguous.

The problem of comparing the technologies in terms of health risk is more difficult than comparing monetary expense but not as hard as comparing environmental impacts. By tallying the number of people who would be killed if either technology A or B were implemented, we can identify which option would achieve our goal at the lowest cost in lives. If no available option offers an acceptably low level of risk, then we ought to give up that goal.

Counting the number of deaths caused by a technology is called "risk analysis," which in practice deals with three kinds of situations, each requiring a different method. The easiest situation is when the technology is routine so that there is reliable information about its risks. For example, automobiles regularly kill nearly 45,000 people per year in the United States. Hazards associated with common occupations and some consumer products are also predictable from year to year (Robertson, 1983). It is a straightforward task to evaluate the effects of new technologies or regulatory policies by looking for changes in these fatality rates.

Catastrophic Accidents

The second situation of concern to risk analysts is the catastrophic accident such as the explosion of the Soviet nuclear reactor at Chernobyl, radiation from which will eventually cause thousands of incidents of cancer across Europe, or the release of poisonous gas from Union Carbide's chemical plant at Bhopal, India, which killed over 3,000 people. These are unique events, so there is little backlog of experience from which to predict with any precision the likelihood of their occurrence or their severity when they do occur. Traditionally, engineers who proposed novel projects with catastrophic potential would design in as many safety features as could be justified in their budgets and would use their best judgments about the likelihood of success. As proponents of their projects, engineers are often overly optimistic, a shortcoming that may explain the frequent failures of many innovative bridges, dams, and airplanes before their designers learn to make them properly (Perrow, 1984; Petroski, 1985).

The modern field of risk analysis was born in the nuclear power industry's attempt to add objectivity—or at least the appearance of objectivity—to traditional engineering judgment about the safety of nuclear reactors (Starr, 1969; Mazur, 1985). Seeking to reassure a wary public that the hazard of a catastrophic release of radiation is very small, the industry sought quantitative estimates of the probability of a core meltdown, the worst kind of accident. Since this had never occurred at a commercial power reactor, such estimates were necessarily hypothetical.

The estimation method used can be illustrated by calculating the probability that a large bell, hung by a rope in a church steeple, will, if the rope fails, kill the bell-ringer standing below. The cautious engineer who designed this installation added as a redundant safety feature a second, similar rope from the bell to the steeple. If the first rope fails, then the second would still hold the bell up. The ringer rings the bell twice a day, each time for thirty minutes. What is the likelihood that he will be killed in a year's time?

We will imagine that this is the first bell ever hung in a church steeple, so the engineer has no experience with bell disasters and must estimate the likelihood of killing the ringer. The only way he can foresee this occurring is for both ropes to fail and for the ringer to be underneath the bell when they do.

The rope manufacturer has made these ropes for years and knows from experience that they break on average once every ten years when holding large loads. Therefore, the probability that either rope will break in one year can be estimated as 0.1. The probability that both ropes will independently break is then 0.1 x 0.1 = 0.01, so the likelihood of the bell falling in any one year is one in a hundred. Even if it does fall, the bell-ringer would be standing in its path only one hour per day (i.e., one-twenty-fourth of the year), so the overall probability that the bell will fall onto the ringer is 0.01 x 1/24, or only 1 chance in 2,400. This seems a low enough risk, so the church's vicar orders the bell installed.

The crux of this method (called "fault-tree analysis") is first to specify combinations of component failures that would lead to a failure of the total system—like the failure of both ropes while the ringer stands below the bell. Then, if the probabilities of these separate component failures are known, they are combined to get the probability of a total system disaster—say one in 2,400. In essence, this is how engineers estimate the probability of a catastrophic reactor meltdown.

The power of this method is impressive; however, it has weaknesses that can lead to estimates of catastrophe that are unrealistic. First, the assumed probability of a rope breaking may be inaccurate. Second, it may be fallacious to assume that the failure of one rope is independent of the failure of the other. Perhaps a rat in the belfry has gnawed on both ropes so that there is a common cause to their failures; in that case, the calculation of 0.1 x 0.1, which assumes the rope failures are unrelated, would underestimate the true probability of the bell falling. Third, there may be paths to disaster that the engineer has overlooked. Perhaps lightning will strike the steeple one stormy night, flowing down the bell's rain-drenched pull cord to electrocute the ringer. For these reasons, the results of such hypothetical risk analyses may not be believable. Indeed, many observers had difficulty reconciling the accident at Three Mile Island with a risk analysis by the nuclear industry only a few years earlier that calculated the probability of such a failure to be minuscule (Rasmussen et al., 1975).

Low-Level Toxins

The third situation where risk analysts try to count deaths is when a population is exposed to a toxic substance, but at too low a dosage to easily see its direct effect. This is a common situation since people are persistently subjected to low levels of radiation and chemicals that are known to be hazardous at higher doses. Many of these exposures are part of the natural environment, such as the cancer-causing radiation in sunlight, or the natural carcinogenic substances in edible plants, or salmonella bacteria in poultry (Ames and Gold, 1989). Other exposures are man-made, including medical x-rays, tobacco smoke, drugs, food additives, and air and water pollution. It is important to assess whether or not damage is being done by these low-level toxins, but this is difficult to do. Just because a synthetic toxin is present does not mean that it has done any harm. Most cancers, birth defects, and other illnesses have "natural" causes, so their occurrence in any population is normal to some extent and does not in itself indicate that any special hazard is present. Furthermore, low-dose carcinogens have "latency periods" of several years between exposure and the appearance of the disease, making it difficult to connect cause with effect.

Problems at the infamous Love Canal illustrate how hard it is to discern if low-level exposures to known toxins actually damage health. Here was a dump site for chemical wastes, some of them carcinogenic. Heavy rains flooded the site after it had been disrupted by construction activity, and chemicals leaked into nearby homes. Residents of the area and journalists became convinced that cancers occurring among the local populace were caused by this chemical leakage, and this has become a part of the popular image of Love Canal. In fact, the cancer rate among Love Canal residents was no higher than elsewhere in New York State (Mazur, 1998).

An ideal way to determine if low doses of a toxin—say, of dioxin, or PCBs, or x-rays—are harmful to people would be to design an experiment that varied the doses. For example, one could randomly assign people to one of four groups, each group containing 1,000 subjects. The first group would be a "control group," receiving no dose of the toxin being tested. The people in the second group would daily receive very small doses of it. Those in the third group would receive, say, twice the dose of the second group; subjects in the fourth group might receive twice the daily dose of the third group. These people would be followed for, say, twenty years—long enough for diseases with long latency periods to emerge. At the end of twenty years, the experimenter would compare the incidences of cancer, birth defects, and other diseases among the four groups. If there were no differences, then one could conclude that the toxin was not harmful at these low levels of exposure. If health damage increased from one group to the next, as exposure increased, then there would be firm evidence showing the damage caused by low exposure to the toxin.

Of course, for both practical and ethical reasons, this experiment can never be run. Such studies are done on mice, and they yield valuable information on the toxicity of substances, but it is uncertain how to generalize the results to humans because mouse bodies operate differently than ours and also because doses that are harmful to little animals may be irrelevant to organisms of our size. We need data on exposure to humans.

"Fortunately" (for science) people have been exposed accidentally or in wartime or in their workplaces to varying levels of many toxins, so it is possible in principle—but difficult in practice—to compare health effects on those with high versus low exposure. For example, Japanese survivors of the atomic bombs had varying levels of radiation exposure, or residents near the Italian town of Seveso were showered with dioxin in 1976 when a nearby chemical plant exploded. These people have been followed for years to see what health effects, if any, occur among them at a greater frequency than among similar people who were not exposed. However, the data obtained this way are far inferior to what would be collected in the ideal experiment described. First, we rarely know accurately how much exposure these people actually received. Also, it is difficult to follow them over the years because people move away and some refuse to cooperate; often, research funding is not available to keep track of everyone. Also, their exposure to the toxin may not be the only thing that differentiates them from the comparison group of unexposed people. For example, if the people of Seveso show an unusually high incidence of birth defects, is that due to their dioxin exposure or might it be caused by some other source—perhaps from bad well water in the town?

These difficulties are so severe that scientists know little about the degree of harm from very low doses of such important chemicals as dioxin, PCBs, sulphur dioxide, DDT, acid rain, and various forms of radiation. As a result, one often hears two competent scientists giving widely divergent estimates of the health effects of, say, radiation from a nuclear power plant, or of chemical food additives or pesticides (Mazur, 2004).

Risks of Generating Electricity

Given the large uncertainties in estimating health risks, how does a risk analyst use these to evaluate technical options? As an illustration, we will compare the damage to health from several methods of generating electricity, based on an analysis by Herbert Inhaber (1979; also see Fritzsche, 1989). Is it more costly in human lives to make electricity from coal, nuclear power, or the sun?

Most electrical generation is based on a simple principle first demonstrated by the scientist Michael Faraday in 1831: electric current flows in a wire when it is moving near a magnet. Large-scale generators are simply huge coils of wire that are rotated between the poles of massive magnets. Electric current produced in the moving coil is sent over distribution wires to consumers. The various generating technologies differ primarily in how they cause the coil of wire to rotate. With hydropower, a waterfall spins the coil; with wind power, breezes spin it. The fossil fuels—coal, oil, and natural gas—are burned, heating water into steam which spins the coil. In a nuclear reactor, atoms of uranium are split (fissioned), releasing from their nuclei much more energy than can be obtained from burning a similar weight of fuel; this energy heats water into steam, which spins the coil.

Photovoltaic solar electricity is the only technology considered here that uses a fundamentally different principle. As in the photoelectric cell of a camera, sunshine falls on a light-sensitive chemical plate, knocking electrons from it to form an electric current.

If we considered only the operation of a generating facility already in place, then obviously coal with its air pollution or nuclear power with its potential for accidents are riskier than a photovoltaic system, which simply collects sunshine. But we must consider the entire generation cycle, including material and fuel production, component fabrication, plant construction, operation and maintenance, transportation, and waste disposition. Remember that solar and wind are low-density energy sources, so a very large array of collectors is needed to obtain the same total energy that is produced from nuclear or fossil fuels in more compact facilities. To build the photovoltaic facility in the first place requires a lot of material for construction, including aluminum, steel, and concrete. Occupational accidents from this material acquisition, transportation, and construction must be counted into the overall risk of the facility.

Hydropower and nuclear power have especially high potentials for catastrophic accidents: dam failures or major releases of radiation such as happened at Chernobyl. How, then, does one compare technology A, which kills one person yearly, with technology B, which usually kills no one but has a one-in-a-thousand (0.001) probability of killing a thousand people in a single accident? Risk analysts handle this by calculating the "expected" number of yearly deaths from rare accidents, defined as the probability that the accident will occur in any year multiplied by the estimated number of deaths if it did occur. For technology B, this would be 0.001 x 1,000 = 1, which is the same as the routine yearly risk from technology A. In effect, the deaths from a rare accident are averaged out over all the years of operation.

Since solar and wind-powered generators work only when sunshine or wind is available, these systems must include some backup source of power that will supply electricity at night or on calm days. Inhaber, our analyst, makes the questionable assumption that the risks from this backup source must be counted as part of the overall risk of the solar or wind system. If one used coal as the backup system, then this alone would account for most of the risk attributable to these renewable sources, which seems a distortion. Here, we assume that the backup system uses natural gas, a very safe fuel that does not add much to the overall risk of solar or wind.

Health damage from energy generation includes workplace disabilities and pollution-related diseases that are not fatal. How should these illnesses be combined with deaths to reckon total health costs? While there is no simple solution, Inhaber and others have equated one fatality to 6,000 person-days lost, as if the average death were equivalent to losing about twenty years of work. This simplifying assumption is made here. (Even if a rather different number is used, the final ranking of technologies does not change much.)

The risk associated with each technology is shown in figure 8.1, where risk is expressed in number of person-days lost per megawatt-year of electricity that is generated. (One megawatt-year supplies all of the annual energy requirements for about 80 Americans.) Since risks of air pollution from fossil fuel burning are not well known, the vertical lines shown in the figure represent ranges of risk to reflect this uncertainty.

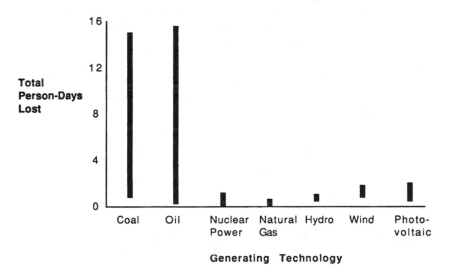

Figure 8.1.   Total person-days lost per megawatt-year of electrical output, for various generating technologies

When the entire energy cycle is considered, solar and wind have appreciable risks, more so than is usually recognized. This is because they are low-density energy sources and therefore must use lots of material per unit of energy output, which in turn causes higher risk to workers. Also, steel is used in some of their fabrication, and coal—used to make most steel—damages health by polluting the air. Most of these costs must be borne before any energy is generated; once solar and wind collectors are in place, they are relatively risk free until the units must be replaced.

Although the full health costs of coal and oil are uncertain, they are almost certainly the riskiest energy sources, producing most of their harm through air pollution. Natural gas burns more cleanly and is one of the safest technologies, despite occasional explosions.

Nuclear power looks surprisingly safe in this comparison, which even counts risks of radioactive waste disposal. The largest part of nuclear power risk comes in construction and fabrication of fuel. During operation, there is no air pollution. Although the potential for a catastrophic accident is present, its estimated probability is very low, so the yearly expected risk—averaged out over the years of operation—is low.

Inhaber's conclusions, so favorable to nuclear power, became controversial as soon as they were published. Antinuclear critics pointed out errors and assumptions in the analysis that if corrected, they claimed, would "completely transform" Inhaber's results (Holdren et al., 1979). Inhaber's major errors have been corrected here, and indeed, nuclear power does not look quite as good, nor renewables as bad, as in his original report. Still, from the standpoint of health risk, nuclear power appears to be one of the safest energy sources, while natural gas seems the best of all.

Before leaving this topic, it is important to recognize significant risk factors that have been left out of the calculations. The risk of nuclear power takes no account of the need to sequester radioactive wastes for thousands of years, nor of the possibility that radioactive material from reactors can, under certain conditions, be converted into weapons. The calculated risk for oil does not include wars fought to protect foreign sources of petroleum, as in Iraq, nor the funding of terrorist activities from the huge oil revenues paid to oil-producing nations in the Middle East.

Environmental Politics

If nuclear power appears safer than other energy-generating technologies that we routinely use, then why is it so controversial? Conversely, if coal is so risky, why is there so little public opposition to its use (Freudenburg and Rosa, 1984)? These are some of the puzzles that surround the politics of environment, which has become so important on both the American agenda and that of the world.

The Politics of Hazard

Since the 1960s, in the industrial democracies, there has been continual public controversy—even mass protests—over technical issues including pesticides, nuclear power, chemical contamination, and toxic waste disposal. The theme that unifies these issues is technological hazard. Protesters charge that various technologies, or the industries and governments that use them, are exposing people to an unacceptable level of risk and that the exposures must be stopped and the risk lessened. Supporters of these technologies respond that the hazards are being exaggerated and that the benefits justify some risk.

Of course, the Rashomon effect is in full play with each side giving inconsistent accounts of the same data and events to justify its position. When a string of technical failures and human errors at the Three Mile Island nuclear reactor caused a partial core meltdown, critics claimed this was very nearly the full-scale disaster they had long warned about: soon another accident would be much worse! Nuclear proponents responded that despite nearly everything going wrong that could, there was little release of radiation and no harm to the public; the safety systems worked! In general, the proponents of a technology overstate its benefits and understate its costs, while opponents do the opposite.

Faced with these inconsistent claims, can we depend on risk analysis for objectively correct answers? Yes and no. For routine hazards where experience has provided reliable data, as with traffic accidents, a fair-minded analyst can provide defensible numbers on the risks of various policy options, for example, the lives saved by wearing seatbelts or driving sober. However, when the risks are hypothetical—a catastrophe in a system with which we have little experience or the harm from some low-level exposure to a diffuse pollutant—there is so much ambiguity in the data and assumptions needed by the analyst that he has ample opportunity to insert his own biases into his calculations and conclusions (Mazur, 1985). Opponents of nuclear power are right to be leery of hypothetical risk analyses produced by nuclear proponents, for they contain the same kind of exaggerations that the opponents themselves use.

Even if risk analyses could be regarded as authoritative, they do not include other costs. One might willingly accept higher health risks from, say, coal instead of nuclear if coal offered compensating benefits. Indeed, coal is cheaper than nuclear power, has no potential for catastrophic accidents, and its spent fuel is not highly radioactive nor can it be used to build nuclear bombs. On the other hand, nuclear power causes no air pollution, does not contribute to greenhouse effect, does not burn a trainload of fuel per day or produce a large volume of ash as waste, and does not require extensive strip mining. Thus, whether Rashomon favors coal or nuclear, or neither or both, there is ample ammunition to justify one position and attack another.

If, by taking all these considerations together, one can make as strong a case for as against nuclear power (or coal), how do people decide their stance? Perhaps a few take the time and trouble to learn all about these options, carefully weighing all pros and cons and eventually reaching a considered solution. Most of us do not; instead we base our positions on incomplete or inaccurate information, ideological predisposition, and subjective "gut" feelings. Often, we adopt the positions of those whom we respect or think of as "people like us," and we reject the positions of those we dislike or already consider as our opponents.

The demands of occupational roles are also important. From the perspective of most employees of a corporate or governmental institution that supports some technology, that institution behaves in a responsible and trustworthy manner and its advocacy of a technology is compatible with—even beneficial to—the public interest; those who oppose the technology may be seen as misguided citizens who do not understand, or simply as troublemakers. A number of factors encourage this perspective. The employee earns his livelihood from the support of the technology (directly or indirectly), his career may be tied to the viability of the technology or at least to the businesses and agencies that support it, and his workday is spent among friends and associates who are like-minded. The common pattern in this situation is to support the policy of one's organization, unless perhaps one is having a particularly bad time on the job, in which case joining the protest may be a convenient outlet.

We can visualize two bright high school students, one choosing a career in engineering and on graduation accepting a job in the electric power industry, the other choosing a career in law and on graduation joining a firm specializing in environmental affairs. Ten years out of high school, they may face each other across the table as adversaries in a power-plant licensing hearing. Why one person chooses engineering while another chooses law is not well understood, although social background variables beyond their own control probably have some influence in career selection. Prior ideological commitments may have led the lawyer into environmental affairs rather than corporate law. But luck and limited job opportunities also channel people to one particular employer rather than another. Once the lawyer and the engineer are embarked on their chosen careers, the professional and organizational influences that led them to their respective sides of the hearing table are not difficult to comprehend.

News coverage that the mass media give to a hazard is another important determinant of how we think about it, or whether we think about it at all. Naturally occurring radon gas in homes is the second leading cause of lung cancer in America, after cigarettes. Yet for only a few years in the mid-1980s did the radon hazard receive a lot of publicity on television and in the newspapers (Mazur, 1987), and only during those years did people worry much about radon in their homes. Many readers of this book will barely have heard of radon, much less worry about it, yet radon remains as hazardous as ever. Public concern about many other environmental issues—toxic waste, greenhouse effect, ozone depletion—rises and falls with the amount of media coverage. If the hazards of coal and oil received as much journalistic attention as they deserve, then probably they, too, would be a focus of public opposition.

The Politics of Scarce Resources

The politics of environmental hazard that emerged after World War II in the industrialized democracies is, in a sense, a luxury afforded by our affluence and freedom. In the Third World, environmental politics are different, focusing more on the management of resources than on the management of hazard. Except for crisis responses to catastrophes like the Bhopal accident in India, little attention is given to technological or environmental risks. The appalling pollution of the Third World's burgeoning cities, far worse than in the relatively clean industrial nations, is not as great a concern as shortages of basic resources: food, arable land, drinkable water, and fuels. Where those necessities are adequate, the focus is on getting richer. The Chinese, who tolerate seven of the ten most air-polluted cities in the world, do not want to close factories that foul the air and water because it would mean a loss of jobs (Hertsgaard, 1999).

Next to satisfying the material wants of their citizens, the major environmental concern of Third World nations is controlling and exploiting their natural resources. Since the outset of colonialization, European powers expropriated mineral and agricultural resources of the regions they controlled. Spain enriched itself and spurred the commercial development of Europe with silver and gold extracted from the New World. Britain imported cotton fiber grown in its Indian and North American colonies and then sold back the spun cloth to these markets, protecting its trade by discouraging the colonies from forming spinning industries of their own.

In the 1920s, American and European oil companies, conforming to the policies of their governments, began pumping oil from the massive petroleum deposits of the Middle East, paying small royalties to the countries there for the right to do so. Although the United States is one of the world's largest oil producers, it was cheaper to import easily accessible oil from the Persian Gulf than to drill at home. By 1970, foreign sources, especially Saudi Arabia and Iran, added considerably to the American oil supply and were even more important for Europe and Japan.

OPEC—the Organization of Petroleum Exporting Countries— was formed in 1960 by the oil-rich countries of the Third World to improve their bargaining power against the giant oil companies of America and Europe. OPEC had little success in its first years, but the Arab-Israeli War of 1973 provided a unique opportunity. After a ceasefire that left Israel occupying Arab territory, OPEC announced that it would embargo oil sales to all industrialized nations that supported Israel. This had the immediate effect of reducing the world supply of oil and thereby escalating its price so that the OPEC members profited greatly (Yergin, 1991).

The cartel eventually lifted its embargo even though the United States held fast to its important alliance with Israel, but by then it was clear that a period of oil scarcity had arrived, marked by escalating energy prices, gasoline rationing, and long lines at filling stations. For the first time, control over a world market in resources had shifted from the industrial nations to OPEC, whose members thereafter limited their production of petroleum to keep it in tight supply, thus maintaining its high price. Then, in 1979, the revolution led by Ayatollah Khomeini in Iran took that major oil producer off the market, and prices shot higher than ever, along with fears that the whole Persian Gulf might be caught up in war.

These shortages of the 1970s were mistakenly interpreted by many people as a sign that the world was running out of oil, an impression reinforced by much publicized forecasts at that time that known reserves of petroleum and natural gas would be used up within a few decades. In fact, the shortages were simply the result of barriers that had been placed in the world's distribution system; there was still plenty of oil in the ground.

Given the very high prices for fuels that prevailed in this period, it became worthwhile for the American and European oil companies to explore and drill for harder-to-reach deposits and for industry, businesses, and the public to limit their energy consumption, not only by turning off lights but by developing more energy-efficient automobiles, appliances, and manufacturing processes. As a result, the world supply of energy increased while demand lessened, so fuel prices dropped.

This was bad news for OPEC because its power depended on controlling the spigot of scarce oil. Held together by economic self-interest, the cartel had within it the potential for disintegration, its members a disparate collection of nations ranging the globe from South America to Asia, mostly Arab but not all, monarchies and socialist governments, some allies of the United States and some enemies. With prices dropping, members violated their production quotas, attempting to bolster falling revenues by selling more oil. The market was glutted, and prices dropped further, breaking OPEC's control. Power reverted to the industrial nations, at least for a time.

With oil prices low again, the industrial nations, especially the United States, reverted to their wasteful ways. If there is one emblem of today's proliferate consumption in America, it is the gas-guzzling SUV, which at this writing accounts for half of new "car" purchases in the United States. In 2004, the United States used more Persian Gulf oil than ever previously, sending huge amounts of money to nations that contain some of our worst (and richest) enemies. Other nations, taking the United States as a model, are now adopting the SUV.

The struggle between the industrialized and the less developed nations for the control of resources is acted out with food as well as oil, although in this case industrial North America holds most of the power (although Brazil is moving to the forefront). During the twentieth century, while the population explosion in the Third World pressed its food supplies, the increase in American farm productivity was astonishing. In 1800, an American farmer needed 5 acres of cropland and 250 hours of labor to produce 100 bushels of wheat. In 1985, it took only 3 acres and 4 hours to grow as much. The reason for this improvement was the industrialization of the farm, including farm machinery, irrigation, chemical fertilizers and pesticides, and scientifically selected seeds and livestock. Today, less than 3 percent of American workers produce enough food to supply the nation amply at low cost, with very large surpluses in storage or sent overseas. Of course, there are costs to this productivity in high energy input, irrigation, depletion of farmland and aquifers, and the pollution of ground water by fertilizer and pesticides.

After World War II, modern farming techniques were transported to some regions of the Third World, producing the so-called "Green Revolution." Since 1950, several Third World nations, notably Mexico, India, and China, have improved their agricultural capabilities to an extent virtually unimaginable at midcentury (Crosson and Rosenberg, 1989). Still, there are food shortages and chronic starvation in some parts of the Third World, especially Sub-Saharan Africa, where Green Revolution techniques have not been very successful. Sometimes food sent for famine relief never reaches those who are starving because of inadequate transportation, corruption, and incompetence or because food shipments are not allowed to cross the lines of civil war. As in the case of oil, the deficiency is not in the total world supply but in failures of the distribution system.

One of the most maddening aspects of the world food situation is that the enormous productive capability of American farmers is purposely held in check while children in the poorest countries are malnourished. Why should this be? The price of food, like that of oil, is dependent on the balance of supply and demand in the world market. World food prices fall when American farmers increase their output. This is good for poor nations that need food but bad for the farmers, for even though they sell more wheat, if the price per bushel has dropped sufficiently, then their total income is down, perhaps even below the break-even point.

Naturally, it is in the farmers' interests to keep food prices high, which usually means limiting the supply of food. American farmers are a "swing vote" in many of the midwestern states, supporting either Republican or Democratic candidates, depending on their farm policies. In this way, the farm lobby has been a potent force protecting food prices. In the 1950s and 1960s, it was actually federal policy to pay farmers to keep some of their land out of production, thus limiting the supply of food so that prices would not fall.

Lest the desire of our farmers to promote higher food prices be regarded as unconscionably selfish, one must see things from their perspective. First of all, American food prices are already quite low, judged by European standards. Second, farmers' incomes are not high compared to those of other occupations (Opie, 1987). Farmers can hardly be expected to work harder, planting more fields, if the likely result is to cut their own income, perhaps even losing their farms. The fault lies not with the farmers but with the way that prices, and ultimately their incomes, are tied to the supply of food. In any case, leaving aside the farmer's own concerns, it would do little good for the American public or the global population if falling prices undermined the world's most productive agricultural system.

The Efficiency Option

The problem is not that we are running out of resources but that it costs so much to procure and use them and sometimes to distribute them where they are most needed. Often, improvements in technology make it cheaper, cleaner, or safer to exploit hard-to-reach deposits, or to cycle through renewables, or to grow more crops; but overall, as the easy pickings are used up, costs of one kind or another rise. If the Third World ever reaches the level of resource consumption that is practiced today in the industrial democracies, the price to be paid in cash, lives, and pollution will be immense.

One promising option for reducing these costs is to use resources more efficiently, reducing the waste in our consumption of energy and products. This includes the conservation of depletable resources, but is not limited to that. Renewable resources must be used more efficiently too. Just because wood can be regrown or the sun and wind are perpetually available does not mean that they can be used without costs. To the contrary, we have seen that their costs are substantial.

The feasibility of increasing energy efficiency in the industrial nations was demonstrated during the oil shortages of the 1970s. Prior to that time, energy was regarded as the essential engine for economic growth: the more fuel consumed, the higher the production of goods and services and the better our lives. Indeed, for decades the increases in American energy consumption per capita were matched by increases in GDP per capita. After 1973, as rising oil prices promoted more efficient use of energy, GDP per capita (in constant dollars) continued to grow while energy consumption leveled off; and by 1985, while economic output was still rising, energy consumption per capita had actually declined. Constantly increasing energy consumption is not essential to maintaining or improving the quality of our lives.

Of course, there is no free lunch; even the efficiency option has costs. One of the United States' most successful measures to conserve oil was the federal requirement that automakers improve the fuel efficiency of new cars. The primary means of doing this was simply to reduce the size and weight of automobiles (Hemphill, 1979). But in case of an accident, occupants are more likely to be killed in a light car than in a heavy one, so here conservation was paid for in lives (Lave, 1981).

On the other hand, efficiency can save lives. An example: The reduction of maximum speed limits from 65 mph to 55 mph, implemented during the 1970s because cars got more mileage per gallon at the slower speed, had the unanticipated effect of reducing highway fatalities. Another example: If the affluent nations would remove red meat from their diets, substituting vegetable sources of protein, they would simultaneously save farm resources and improve their health. It is inefficient to grow crops to feed livestock that are then eaten by people for protein. By eating soybeans or other protein crops directly, people would get the same dietary value using less land, water, and fertilizer; and by eliminating red meat, the risk of heart disease is reduced.

Efficiency, like any other option, has costs and benefits that must be traded off. Some schemes for conservation will be worthwhile, others will not. But overall, decreasing resource consumption by improving efficiency is our best bet for making a cleaner, healthier environment in the industrial nations; and it would provide the developing nations with a saner, safer, less wasteful model to which they might aspire.

9

Prospects

A book devoted to global problems can be depressing, yet in many ways the world's prospects are fairly good. We worry about terrorist attacks, a replay of 9/11 or worse, and we continue to fight conventional wars in distant lands, but we no longer fear the dreadful consequences of a full-scale nuclear exchange between the United States and the Soviet Union. Today, more people are leading freer, healthier, and more prosperous lives than ever before. The challenge is to preserve these benefits for the future and to spread them to the poorer nations while eliminating pockets of poverty that still exist in the affluent ones. We live in a time of incredible scientific and technological achievements; but these must be harnessed more intelligently, maximizing their benefits and minimizing their costs. Population is growing too quickly in the Third World, but fertility is dropping rapidly in most places except Sub-Saharan Africa, and if this change is encouraged with wise policies, the earth's population may level off in the next fifty years at an acceptable number. There are as many signs here for hope as for despair.

The Western Sanctuary

By the beginning of the twentieth century, there was no longer much likelihood of civil war among the American states, or of a continental war between the United States and Canada. This peaceful coalescence was produced by a growing web of economic and legal interdependencies and especially by the extensive trade, travel, and other communications networks that united previously separate regions of North America. Across areas sharing the English language, there was rapid convergence in cultures and lifestyles so that the sense of difference and alienation that had separated, say, the North from the South after the Civil War, gave way to a new sense of shared identity, not wholly nationalistic, for it even crossed the Canadian border.

As people of different regions became increasingly similar to one another in attitudes, habits, and ways of life and as cross-country commerce and travel increased, North America (except Mexico) became a sanctuary in the sense that warfare within the continental boundaries was implausible. There remained differences and competition between regions, but war was psychologically excluded as a response to these rivalries, not because of any overarching police power that prohibited it, but simply because it was unthinkable that one would fire cannon between, say, Kentucky and Tennessee.

The North American consensus during the world wars reflected the continent's shared identity, which extended at least to Britain among the European nations. Wartime experiences reinforced that identity, as typically happens among people who coalesce against a common enemy. However, war was not the essential cause of the convergence, which proceeded apace during decades when there was no external enemy of consequence. The shared culture and language, combined with increasing interdependencies, communication, and personal travel, were sufficient to solidify and extend these bonds.

North America was not the only area of the world to encompass once warring subregions into a placid sanctuary. The European Union, originally based on the burying of hatchets between France and Germany, is more remarkable for the rapidity with which war has become outmoded between its member nations. We may also include countries outside Europe or North America: Israel, Australia, New Zealand, and perhaps Japan and South Korea.

It is crucial to stress that these are not temporary coalitions, as have been based in the past on balances of power, which easily disintegrate. Bonds among the industrial democracies, increasingly based upon common culture and shared identity, including the rapid spread of English as a first or second language, and reinforced by tightly connected economic and legal dependencies, are likely to be enduring. The nuclear arsenals of the United States, France, Britain, and Israel are not perceived as directly threatening to each other or to any other nation in the Western Sanctuary, and there are no apparent fears that this situation will deteriorate.

It is ironic that this increasing sharing of identity holds more strongly across the educated classes of the industrial democracies than it does between the rich and poor of any single society. Academicians and other professionals know from their own experiences how easy it is to find common interests and close rapport with foreign colleagues over shared drinks and dinner after business or conference hours. There is little difficulty in making conversation—usually in English—about music, clothes, food, sex, and current events. Yet typically these people have no such common ground or rapport with the poor and uneducated of their own nations. Whatever negative connotations one may draw from this observation, it is nonetheless reassuring that since educated elites are usually the ones who initiate warfare between industrial nations, they—if not the underclasses—identify with one another.

A critical policy goal for the United States ought to be to maintain cooperative solidarity with others in the sanctuary and to extend its boundaries farther. The most important additions to the fold would be those bogeymen of the Cold War era, Russia and China. We have the opportunity. Both of these former adversaries now have cooperative relations with the West, but these are fragile links that require nurturing. They should move toward democratic institutions and full civil rights for their citizens, while we should tolerate slower than ideal progress toward these goals. The United States and China now have an excellent (and substantial) trading relationship, notwithstanding China's maintenance of an authoritarian government, showing that despite these nations' contradictory political values, there are plenty of incentives to remain in each other's good graces. We must hope that the persistent tension between mainland China and Taiwan soon defuses, as it has the potential to explode into war, forcing the United States to support Taiwan.

Incorporating the Third World

The addition of China and Russia, and the former Soviet satellite nations, to the Western Sanctuary, would make most of the Northern Hemisphere a (relatively) war-free zone of cooperation. That zone, unfortunately, omits half the world's population. The prospects then range from optimistic to awful.

In the worst case, we could see a polarization between the industrialized nations and the Third World, perhaps impelled by antagonism between radical Islamists and Western Christians, with leaders on both sides believing that they are instruments of God. Imagine the nightmare of Osama bin Laden's followers taking power in Pakistan and getting control of that nation's nuclear arsenal. No doubt the industrial powers would inflict far more harm to Third World nations than vice versa, but the North could lose cities to surreptitiously planted atomic bombs, or to chemical or biological attacks.

There is plenty of potential for catastrophic war *between* Third World nations, which are rife with conflicts of interest and ethnic hostilities. Pakistan and India have fought three wars since their independence from Britain, and now both sides have nuclear weapons, as do a small but growing number of other Third World nations.

There are more optimistic scenarios, especially those based on improving lifestyles in the Third World, more sharing of cultural values, and more tolerance for values that are not shared. Recent modernizations of South Korea and Taiwan show that it is possible for poor nations to enter the privileged circle of the industrial democracies. But the rarity with which this occurs is dismaying.

Certainly the rich nations can facilitate this transition. Obvious steps are for the European Union to accept Turkey into membership, for both America and Europe to press the Israelis and Palestinians to settle their ongoing conflict, and for the United States to forego spurious interference in Third World politics.

A promising project for the United States and Canada is to incorporate Latin America into their zone of affluence. The North American Free Trade Agreement (NAFTA) of 1994, which combines Mexico, Canada, and the United States into a relatively free trade zone, was a move in this direction. This is a realistic goal, given that Latin America is already the most advanced region of the Third World in terms of lifestyle and political freedom (while least equitable in distribution of income and wealth). It would be essential for the Latin Americans to share their benefits more equally among their citizens than they do at present. Perhaps the European Union might extend a similar hand to its southern neighbor, Africa, although prospects there are far dimmer than in Latin America.

Except in regions of the Third World that are absolutely resistant to—and appalled by—Western values, we may expect continued homogenization of cultures across the globe. This uniformity is propelled by three engines: mass communication, mass marketing, and personal travel. In past decades, all of these have been growing at rates that seem exponential, facilitated by new technologies and falling real costs. There is no need to dwell on satellite telecommunications that allow all of the countries of the world simultaneously to view a televised event as it happens, or the ease and relative cheapness of intercontinental air travel and of telephone calling and the internet, or the flood of consumer goods in response to demand promoted by mass advertising. It is obvious enough that these modern forces are building a montage of shared lifestyles and tastes, ever changing in time but extending across distances to every country that is wealthy enough to adopt it. It may be dismaying to recognize that pop culture is sweeping the world, but there will be dividend enough if it contributes to an end result of peaceful coexistence.

Any realistic program for Third World development requires a serious commitment of resources from the rich nations, especially the United States. The Third World itself must take effective control of its population problem growth, slowing to China's level, although hopefully avoiding China's sometimes severe methods. While natural processes may now be lowering birthrates, these are insufficient, especially in Africa, and must be reinforced with policies of planned birth control. Unfortunately, the Catholic Church and Protestant fundamentalists in the United States continue to thwart some of the most effective means of population control. Hand-in-hand with birth control must be improved medical care, notably for victims of HIV infection but also for afflictions as simple to treat or prevent as malaria and childhood diarrhea.

Development of the Third World implies increased industrialization and consumption, which means more pollution and depletion of easily accessible resources. Almost certainly, the environmental problems of the Third World will get worse before they get better because the people themselves regard these problems as less important than the provision of food, shelter, and jobs for a growing labor force and the improvement of material lifestyle. It has only been within the past few decades, after reaching an unprecedented level of material comfort, that people of the industrial democracies have brought environmental pollution and technological hazards onto their political agendas, rectifying some of the damage of their roughshod ride to affluence. Why should the people of less developed countries be any different?

For example, Brazil's vast rain forest is rapidly disappearing, partly because large agricultural interests are clearing the land but also because numerous small farmers yearly burn sections of it so they can plant their crops. From the viewpoint of world ecology, the preservation of this rain forest is of primary importance. Its growing vegetation absorbs carbon dioxide from the air, alleviating the greenhouse effect, and it is home to an enormous number of plant and animal species, which are becoming extinct as the forest disappears. But the poor farmers have hungry families to support, and from their viewpoint there is no better option available than to clear a small space in the immense forest to grow enough crops for the year. With what justice does an American demand of Brazil that it preserve the rain forest when America has cut down much of its own forests? Perhaps the fairer course is to replant trees across the United States.

China's situation is similar to that of Brazil. Its enormous coal deposits are an obvious source of fuel for China's further development, cheap and already at hand, but coal burning is one of the worst contributors to greenhouse effect. Can the already developed countries ask or expect China to forgo the use of its coal for the sake of global warming? Will the developed nations donate to China an alternate source of energy, perhaps natural gas, that is more benign to the environment?

It is especially the affluent nations that should reduce their wasteful consumption, first, because they have so much fat to cut away, and second, because they have already used more than their share of world resources and have produced more than their share of pollution. Yet we resist even the simple solutions for some of our most blatant inefficiencies. Businessmen wear ties and jackets in summer so that offices must be overly air-conditioned for comfort. Communities in the arid southwestern United States daily sprinkle lawns with scarce water rather than landscaping in a way that is appropriate for the dry climate. The U.S. Postal Service offers discount rates encouraging advertisers to send 7.5 billion pounds of "junk mail" yearly, of which 95 percent is thrown away unopened, clogging the already overtaxed garbage disposal system. New upper-middle-class homes in America, designed for a single family, commonly have nine or more rooms (plus baths) and 3,000 feet of living area, requiring perhaps three times as much energy for heating, lighting, and air conditioning as the average American home and perhaps ten times what is needed for a Japanese home. Today, the mean size of the American family is only 3.2 members, but it owns on average more than two cars and nearly three televisions. This exorbitant level of consumption could be reduced without any serious loss in material lifestyle, lessening the environmental costs of resource utilization and providing the less developed world with a more attainable goal.

Managing the Earth

The Earth is becoming a smaller place, and its parts are now so highly interconnected that an event in one region often has quick and serious repercussions around the globe. No longer can nations or other major entities be left wholly to mind their own business, for what one does affects the rest. As human activities alter the climate, punch holes in the ozone layer of the upper atmosphere, foul the oceans, drive species to extinction, and change the surface of the continents, the time has come to manage the Earth's environment in a rational way, manipulating human impacts so as to minimize their damage and to preserve the fruits of the Earth for future generations.

The notion of managing the Earth will disturb those who believe that nature should remain "natural"—untamed and forever wild. But the scale of human activity is now so large that we are altering the planetary environment willy-nilly, in a chaotic and destructive way. I cannot envision a plausible future in which human interference shrinks to insignificance, for pollution is a necessary cost of nearly all of our activities. If all polluters have their own way, and there is no coordinated activity to prevent further harm and to cure the damage already done, then the Earth's surface will be ruined.

To manage the planet wisely, as today's governments attempt for their own territories, is an awesome but necessary prospect. The Montreal Protocol of 1987, an international agreement limiting the worldwide release of chlorofluorocarbons into the atmosphere to reduce the destruction of the stratospheric ozone layer by these compounds, was a small step in this direction. There has been no comparable success in managing greenhouse gases, mostly because of American recalcitrance. The political problems of reconciling conflicting interests on a global scale will be enormous, but remember that the task of managing thirteen bickering American colonies seemed nearly insurmountable in the eighteenth century. Perhaps in the twenty-first century, world management will become the routine task of bureaucrats and elected politicians.

World managers will have to deal with technical experts, and this presents a new kind of problem not known to America's founding fathers but which has emerged as the industrial nations tried to cope with their own environmental issues. Few citizens or politicians understand the science and technology that underlie issues of environmental pollution and technological hazard. Unlike traditional matters with which legislators and bureaucrats concern themselves, these require technical training to grasp. Even the best educated in our populace have little knowledge of science. The ozone layer, greenhouse warming, nuclear power plants, dioxin, PCBs—these are mysterious issues to most people who have little understanding of the processes that cause harm or suggest a solution.

Worsening matters is the public misconception of science as being objective and pat. People with this mistaken notion expect any two scientists to arrive at the same answer when asked such factual questions as: How likely is it that this exposure to PCBs will cause cancer? Or, what is the probability of a reactor meltdown at a nuclear power plant? Yet our newspapers continually report situations where one scientist says the chance is high of getting cancer, while another says it is low. One expert says a technology is completely safe, and another warns that it may cause a catastrophe at any time.

This is Rashomon in scientific garb, decked out with graphs and regression equations, electrophoreses and fault-tree analyses. Each interest group has its technical experts, like lawyers in a courtroom, who defend its own position and undermine the arguments of the opposition. But unlike lawyers, scientists are constrained by fact. How, then, can one see black where another sees white?

Some scientific principles are so well established that their application in routine matters is cut and dried, but issues of current scientific research are not so well understood. For example, scientists do not know why certain chemicals and radiation cause cancer, nor do they know very well how potent these cancer causers are at very low doses because they lack good data on exposure to humans. These are topics of ongoing study.

Consider an example of scientific ambiguity, this one simple enough to be appreciated by a layperson. Given the inconclusive nature of available data, it is possible to postulate several different relationships between the amount of radiation exposure to a population and the resultant increase in a cancer like leukemia. There are two commonly assumed "dose-effect curves" relating dose of radiation to the incidence of cancer. These are the "linear" and the "threshold" curves (figure 9.1). Most interesting for our purposes is how such scientific ambiguities enter into political controversies over technology, such as whether or not to build nuclear power plants. In the early years of the nuclear controversy, when there was much argument over the harm that might be done by the low level of radiation released from a normally operating nuclear plant, scientists were divided over which dose-effect curve to apply. Those favoring nuclear power often used the threshold curve because it implies that a very low level of routine radiation—below the threshold—causes no harm to the public. Opposition scientists preferred the linear curve, which implies that any amount of radiation, no matter how slight, is harmful (Mazur, 2004).

The same Rashomon-like interpretations of a scientific ambiguity occurred in the 1990s during the debate about the greenhouse effect. Good measurements over several decades showed the concentration of carbon dioxide in the atmosphere to be continually increasing. Measurements of the average temperature of Earth's atmosphere showed a general warming, but here the trend was not as regular. Figure 9.2 displays one of the best of these long trend lines, plotting the yearly average temperature of the atmosphere since 1880, the earliest year that comparable measurements are available. The graph shows the global temperature moving generally upward over the past century. However, there was an unexplained reversal from 1940 to 1970 while CO_2 was increasing in the atmosphere. This bothered some scientists, who regarded the global warming theory as unnecessarily alarming. Others disregarded the 1940–1970 period as a short-term anomaly, emphasizing the long-term warming.

How do managers and the public decide environmental policy in the face of this kind of ambiguity? Reducing CO_2 in the at-

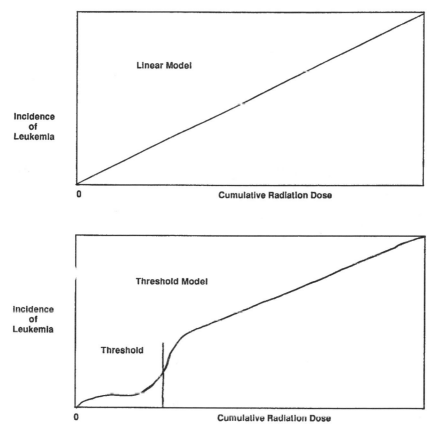

Figure 9.1. Comparison of linear and threshold models

mosphere means cutting back on fossil fuel consumption, a costly action. Is it warranted in the face of this uncertainty?

Fortunately in this case, under United Nations auspices, a scientific task force was formed in 1988, including atmospheric scientists from nations around the world. Called the Intergovernmental Panel on Climate Change (IPCC), it continually assesses ongoing scientific research and periodically reports the best scientific picture currently available. IPCC evaluations report with increasing confidence that global warming is a continuing trend and that at least a portion of it is caused by human-produced consumption of fossil fuels. There remains uncertainty about the timing and degree of warming and how it will affect different regions of the world.

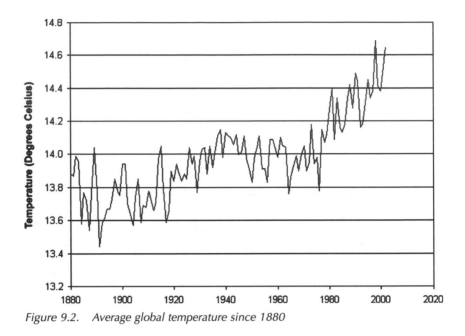

Figure 9.2. Average global temperature since 1880

But the basic case is virtually certain. Today, only the most contrarian scientists reject this conclusion.

Sometimes it is simply the most vocal or visible expert who wins the attention of the press and therefore the public, even though his or her view may be a minority position in the community of experts. When technical experts disagree, how are we to know which one to believe? The only people who can resolve technical disputes between experts are other experts, because in most instances their special knowledge is required to understand the nature of the disagreements. We must, then, depend on the unusual skills of this elite. But although experts have special technical knowledge, they do not have special wisdom to guide our world for us, and they certainly do not have the mandate to govern, which is the basic right of the people in a democracy. Here then is a peculiarly modern dilemma. How can democratic governments use the special knowledge of technical experts—who often disagree among themselves—to manage the world without surrendering to them the power to govern?

References

Achebe, C. 1959. *Things Fall Apart*. New York: Ballantine Books.

Ames, B., and L. Gold. 1989. "Misconceptions Regarding Environmental Pollution and Cancer Causation," pp. 19–34 in *Health Risks and the Press*, edited by M. Moore. Washington, D.C.: The Media Institute.

Amnesty International. 1987. *Amnesty International Report, 1987*. London: Amnesty International Publications.

Aveni, A. 1989. *Empires of Time*. New York: Basic Books.

Avigad, N. 1974. "Jericho," pp. 113–20 in *Archaeology*. Jerusalem: Keter.

Bairoch, P. 1982. "International Industrialization Levels from 1750 to 1980," *Journal of European Economic History* 11.

Baum, J. 1987. "Baby Makes Three—and No More." *Christian Science Monitor* (20 August): 16–17.

Bergen, P. *Holy War, Inc.* New York: Free Press.

Berlin, B., and P. Kay. 1969. *Basic Color Terms*. Berkeley: University of California Press.

Boorstin, D. 1983. *The Discoverers*. New York: Random House.

Braungart, R., and M. Braungart. 1983. "Terrorism," pp. 299–337 in *Prevention and Control of Aggression*, edited by A. Goldstein. New York: Pergamon.

Breyer, S. 1993. *Breaking the Vicious Circle*. Cambridge, Mass.: Harvard University Press.

Brown, L., and J. Jacobson. 1986. *Our Demographically Divided World*. Washington, D.C.: Worldwatch Institute.

Bureau of the Census. 1960. *Historical Statistics of the United States, Colonial Times to 1957*. Washington, D.C.: U.S. Government Printing Office.

Burnett, W., and S. Ban. 1989. "Changing Prospects for Natural Gas in the United States." *Science* 244: 305–10.

Caldwell, J., and P. Caldwell. 1990. "High Fertility in Sub-Saharan Africa." *Scientific American* 262 (May): 118–25.

Cardwell, D. 1972. *Turning Points in Western Technology, A Study of Technology, Science, and History*. New York: Neale Watson.

Case, K., and R. Fair. 1989. *Principles of Economics*. Englewood Cliffs, N.J.: Prentice-Hall.

Chandler, T., and G. Fox. 1974. *3000 Years of Urban Growth*. New York: Academic Press.

Chang, J., and J. Halliday. 2006. *Mao*. London: Random House.

Chow, G. 1987. "Development of a More Market-Oriented Economy in China," *Science* 235: 295–99.

CIA. 2004. *World Factbook 2004*. Washington D.C.

Crosson, P., and N. Rosenberg. 1989. "Strategies for Agriculture?" *Scientific American* 261 (September): 128–35.

Davies, N. 1996. *Europe: A History*. New York: Oxford University Press.

Deevey, E. 1960. *Scientific American* (September): 198.

Dobbs, M. 1997. *Down with Big Brother: The Fall of the Soviet Empire*. New York: Alfred A. Knopf.

Doblhoffer, E. 1973. *Voices in Stone*. New York: Granada.

Doll, R., and R. Peto. 1981. *The Causes of Cancer*. New York: Oxford University Press.

Dominici, P. 2004. *A Brighter Tomorrow*. New York: Rowman & Littlefield.

Economic Report of the President, 1989. 1989. Washington, D.C.: U.S. Government Printing Office.

Ehrlich, P. 1968. *The Population Bomb*. New York: Ballantine Books.

Ehrlich, P., and A. Ehrlich. 1970. *Population Resources Environment*. San Francisco: W. H. Freeman.

Environmental Protection Agency. 1987. *Unfinished Business: A Comparative Assessment of Environmental Problems*. Washington, D.C.: Office of Policy, Planning and Evaluation.

Estes, R. 1984. *The Social Progress of Nations*. New York: Praeger.

Fallows, J. 1981. *National Defense*. New York: Random House.

Flavin, C., and C. Pollock. 1985. "Harnessing Renewable Energy," pp. 172–99 in *State of the World 1985*, edited by L. Brown et al. New York: W. W. Norton.

Freedman, R. 1979. "Theories of Fertility Decline: A Reappraisal," pp. 63–79 in *World Population and Development*, edited by P. Hauser. Syracuse, N.Y: Syracuse University Press.

Freudenburg, W., and E. Rosa. 1984. *Public Reactions to Nuclear Power: Are There Critical Masses?* Boulder, Colo.: Westview. [Published by Westview Press for the American Association for the Advancement of Science, Washington, D.C.]

Friedman, T. 2002. *New York Times,* January 23.

Friedrich, O., R. Chavra, and D. Devoss. 1984. "A Proud Capital's Distress." *Time* (August 6): 26–35.

Fritzsche, A. 1989. "The Health Risks of Energy Production," *Risk Analysis* 9: 565–77.

Fursenko, A., and T. Naftali. 1997. *One Hell of a Gamble.* New York: W. W. Norton.

Gelb, I. 1963. *A Study of Writing.* Chicago: University of Chicago Press.

Gibbons, J. H., P. D. Blair, and H. L. Gwin. 1989. "Strategies for Energy Use." Scientific American 261(3): 136–44.

Gorbachev, M. 1987. *Perestroika: New Thinking for Our Country and the World.* Cambridge, Mass.: Harper & Row.

Greenberg, J. 1983. "Languages of the World." *Encyclopedia Americana,* Vol. 16. Danbury, Conn.: Grolier.

Gregory, R. 1966. *Eye and Brain.* New York: McGraw-Hill. *Guinness Book of World Records.* 1985.

Hanley, C. 1986. "War in Year of Peace." *Syracuse Herald-American* (October 26): El.

Hansen, J., and S. Lebedeff. 1988. "Global Surface Air Temperatures: Update Through 1987." *Geophysical Research Letters,* 15 (April): 323–26.

Hauser, P. 1979. *World Population and Development.* Syracuse. N.Y.: Syracuse University Press.

Hemphill, J.R. 1979. "Energy Conservation in the Transportation Sector," pp. 79–96 in *Energy Conservation and Public Policy,* edited by J. Sawhill. Englewood Cliffs, N.J.: Prentice-Hall.

Henderson, D. 1988. "Smallpox: Never Again," pp. 226–29 in *Global Issues 88/89,* edited by R. Jackson. Guilford, Conn.: Dushkin.

Hertsgaard, M. 1999. *Earth Odyssey.* New York: Broadway Books.

Hitchcock, W. 2003. *The Struggle for Europe.* New York: Doubleday.

Hobsbawm, E. 1962. *The Age of Revolution 1789–1848.* New York: New American Library.

———. 1969. *Industry and Empire: An Economic History of Britain Since 1750.* Baltimore: Penguin Books.

Holdren, J., K. Smith, and G. Morris. 1979. "Energy: Calculating the Risks (II)." *Science* 204: 564–67.

Hough, J., and M. Fainsod. 1979. *How the Soviet Union Is Governed.* Cambridge, Mass.: Harvard University Press.

Humana, C. 1986. *World Human Rights Guide*. New York: Facts on File.
Inhaber, H. 1979. "Risk with Energy from Conventional and Nonconventional Sources." *Science* 203: 718–23.
Jacobs, J. 1982. *The Moral Justification of Suicide*. Springfield, Ill.: Charles C Thomas.
Johanson, D., and M. Edey. 1981. *Lucy*. New York: Simon & Schuster.
Johnson, P. 1983. *Modern Times*. New York: Harper & Row.
Keegan, J. 1999. *The First World War*. New York: Alfred A. Knopf.
Kennedy, P. 1987. *The Rise and Fall of the Great Powers*. New York: Random House.
Kennedy, R. 1971. *Thirteen Days*. New York: W. W. Norton.
Kerblay, B. 1983. *Modern Soviet Society*. New York: Pantheon Books.
Kerr, R. 1989. "Hansen vs. the World on the Greenhouse Threat." *Science* 244: 1041–43.
Keyfite, N. 1989. The Growing Human Population." *Scientific American* 261 (September): 119–26.
Kinder, H., and W. Hiloemann. 1974. *The Anchor Atlas of World History*, Vols. I and II. Garden City. N. Y.: Doubleday.
Koestler, A. 1960. *The Watershed*. Garden City, N.Y.: Doubleday.
Kolata, G. 1999. *Flu*. New York: Farrar, Straus and Giroux.
Kurian, G. 1984. *The New Book of World Rankings*. New York: Facts on File.
Kurosawa, A. 1950. *Rashomon: A Film by Akira Kurosawa*. New York: Grove Press.
Landis, D. 1998. The Wealth and Poverty of Nations: Why Some Are So Rich and Some So Poor. New York: W. W. Norton.
Lave, L. 1981. "Conflicting Objectives in Regulating the Automobile." *Science* 202: 893.
Lewis, B. 2002. *What Went Wrong*. New York: Oxford University Press.
Manchester, W. 1973. *The Glory and the Dream*. Boston: Little, Brown.
———. 1978. *American Caesar: Douglas MacArthur, 1880–1964*. New York: Dell.
Mangin, W. 1967. "Squatter Settlements," *Scientific American* 217 (October): 3–11.
Mazur, A. 1985. "Bias in Risk-Benefit Analysis," *Technology in Society* 7: 25–30.
———. 1987. "Putting Radon on the Public's Risk Agenda," *Science, Technology, & Human Values* 12 (Summer–Fall): 86–93.
———. 1998. *A Hazardous Inquiry*. Cambridge, Mass.: Harvard University Press.
———. 2004. *True Warnings and False Alarms*. Washington D.C.: Resources for the Future.

———. 2005. *Biosociology of Dominance and Deference*. New York: Rowman & Littlefield.

Mazur, A., and L. Robertson. 1972. *Biology and Social Behavior*. New York: Free Press.

Mazur, A., and E. Rosa. 1974. "Energy and Life-Style." *Science* 186: 607–10.

McCombs, M., and D. Shaw. 1972. "The Agenda-Setting Function of the Mass Media," *Public Opinion Quarterly* 36: 235–43.

McDowell, B. 1984. "Mexico City: An Alarming Giant," National Geographic 166 (August): 138–72.

McEvedy, C. 1984. *The Macmillan World History Factfinder*. New York: Macmillan.

McKeown, T. 1976. *The Modern Rise of Population*. London: Edward Arnold.

Milgram, S. 1974. *Obedience to Authority*. New York: Harper & Row.

Milnar, J. 1987. "Emigres Rarely Unhappy with Life Back in the USSR, Interviews Show." *Syracuse Post-Standard* (February 18): A-3.

Morris, C. 1980. "Andean South America: from Village to Empire," pp. 391–97 in *The Cambridge Encyclopedia of Archaeology*, edited by A. Sherratt. New York: Cambridge University Press.

Nagle, J. 1989. *Introduction to Comparative Politics*, 2nd ed. Chicago: Nelson-Hall.

New York Times News Service. 1989. "20% of Soviets Live in Poverty, Authorities Say," *Syracuse Herald-American* (January 29): A4.

Nisbet, E., and J. Shanahan. 2004. *MSRG Special Report: Restrictions on Civil Liberties, Views of Islam, & Muslim Americans*. Media & Society Research Group, Cornell University (December).

Opie, J. 1987. *The Law of the Land*. Lincoln: University of Nebraska Press.

Perlez, J. 1988. "Sudan Racked by Famine, Agrees to U.S. Food Airlift." *The New York Times* (October 13): A1.

———. 1990. "East-Bloc's Admirers in Africa Draw Line at Multiparty Politics," *The New York Times* (May 22): 11.

Perrow, C. 1984. *Normal Accidents*. New York: Basic Books.

Petroski, H. 1985. *To Engineer Is Human*. New York: St. Martin's.

Pfeifer, J. 1982. *The Creative Explosion*. New York: Harper & Row.

Pierre, A. 1982. *The Global Politics of Arms Sales*. Princeton, N.J.: Princeton University Press.

Pipes, R. 1984. *Survival Is Not Enough*. New York: Simon & Schuster.

Preston, D. 2000. *The Boxer Rebellion*. New York: Berkley Publishing.

Rasmussen, W., et al. 1975. *Reactor Safety Study, Report WASH-1400*. Washington, D.C.: Nuclear Regulatory Commission.

Reeves, R. 1988. "Capital of Communism Stands as Monument to System's Failure." *Syracuse Herald-American* (May 22): E3.

Richie, D. 1972. *Focus on Rashomon*. Englewood Cliffs, N.J.: Prentice-Hall.

Roberts, J. 1996. *The Penguin History of Europe*. London: Penguin Books.

Roberts, P. 2004. *The End of Oil*. Boston: Houghton Mifflin.

Robertson, L. 1983. *Injuries—Causes, Control Strategies, and Public Policy*. Lexington, Mass.: Lexington Books.

Roosevelt, T. 1926. "A Colonial Survival," pp. 300–316 in *Literary Essays*. New York: Scribners.

Rouse, W. (trans.). 1938. *Homer: The Iliad*. New York: New American Library.

Schneider, S. 1989. "The Greenhouse Effect: Science and Policy," *Science* 243: 771–81.

Schurr, S., et al. 1979. *Energy in America's Future*. Baltimore: Johns Hopkins University Press.

Scott, W. 1962. *Ivanhoe*. New York: New American Library.

Select Committee on Intelligence. 2006. *Postwar Findings about Iraq's WMD Program and Links to Terrorism and How They Compare with Prewar Assessment*. Washington D.C: U.S. Senate, September 8.

Shils, E., and M. Janowitz. 1948. "Cohesion and Disintegration in the Wehrmacht in World War II," *Public Opinion Quarterly* 12 (Summer): 280–315.

Shipler, D. 1983. *Russia: Broken Idols, Solemn Dreams*. New York: Penguin Books.

Shirer, W. 1960. *The Rise and Fall of the Third Reich*. New York: Simon & Schuster.

Simons, E. 1989. "Human Origins," *Science* 245: 1343–50.

Smith, H. 1976. *The Russians*. New York: Ballantine Books.

Smolowe, J. 1989. "Deng's Big Lie," *Time* (June 26): 32–33.

Starr, C. 1969. "Social Benefit versus Technological Risk." *Science* 165: 1232–38.

Stouffer, S., et al. 1949. *The American Soldier*. Princeton, N.J.: Princeton University Press.

Stout, D., and J. Cushman, Jr. 2004. "Defense Missile for U.S. System Fails to Launch," *New York Times* (December 12).

Strayer, J., and H. Gatzke. 1984. *The Mainstream of Civilization*. New York: Harcourt Brace Jovanovich.

Talbott, S. 1970. *Khrushchev Remembers*. Boston: Little, Brown.

———. 1974. *Khrushchev Remembers: The Last Testament*. Boston: Little, Brown.

Taubman, W. 2003. *Khrushchev*. New York: W. W. Norton.

Taylor, C. L., and D. Jodice. 1983. *World Handbook of Political and Social Indicators*. New Haven: Yale University Press.

Tocqueville, A. 1946. *Democracy in America*. New York: Oxford University Press.

Toland, J. 1976. *Adolf Hitler*. New York: Ballantine Books.

Toriumi, Y. 1973. "A New Role for Japan," pp. 293–318 in *Half the World*, edited by Arnold Toynbee. New York: Holt, Rinehart and Winston.

Tuck, J., and R. Grenier. 1985. "Discovery in Labrador: A 16th-Century Basque Whaling Port." *National Geographic* 168 (July): 40–68.

Tuchman, B. 1962. *The Guns of August*. New York: Macmillan.

———. 1984. *The March of Folly: From Troy to Vietnam*. New York: Ballantine Books.

United Nations. 2004. *World Urbanization Prospects, The 2003 Revision*. New York: United Nations.

United Nations Development Programme. 2003. *Human Development Report 2003*. New York: United Nations.

Uris, L. 1961. *Mila 18*. New York: Doubleday.

U.S. Arms Control and Disarmament Agency. 1983–1987. *World Military Expenditures and Arms Transfers*. Washington, D.C.: U.S. Government Printing Office.

U.S. Home Heating Fire Patterns and Trends Through 1987–1989. Quincy, Mass.: National Fire Protection Association.

Van Den Berghe, P. 1973. *Age and Sex in Human Societies*. Belmont, Calif.: Wadsworth.

Walzer, M. 1977. *Just and Unjust Wars*. New York: Basic Books.

Weeks, J. 1986. *Population*. Belmont. Calif.: Wadsworth.

Westoff, C. 1986. "Fertility in the United States," *Science* 234: 554–59.

Whipple, C. 1980. "The Energy Impacts of Solar Heating," *Science* 208: 262–66.

Wilson, J., and R. Herrnstein. 1985. *Crime and Human Nature*. New York: Simon & Schuster.

Winston, D. 1979. "There Goes the Sun," *Newsweek* (December 3): 35.

Wolff, E. 1987. "Estimates of Household Wealth Inequality in the U.S., 1962—1983," *The Review of Income and Wealth* 33 (September): 231–56.

Yaukey, D. 1985. *Demography*. New York: St. Martin's.

Yeager, C., and L. Janos. 1985. *Yeager: An Autobiography*. New York: Bantam Books.

Yergin, D. 1991. *The Prize: The Epic Quest for Oil, Money, and Power*. New York: Simon & Schuster.

Index

ABMs. *See* anti-ballistic missiles
Acheulean tool culture, 15
acid rain, 177
Afghanistan, 117, 125
Afghan War, 79, 83–84
Africa: European colonization, 59. *See also* Sub-Saharan Africa
age-sex structure, of populations, 160–62
agrarian societies: ancient civilizations, 20–25; birth and death rates in, 148–49; fertility and family size in, 156–57; general description of, 41–42; women's status in, 157
Agrarian/Urban Transformation: as a natural progression from initial conditions, 32–35; cultural zones, 35–39; defined, 19; diffusion of culture and, 25–26; emergence of civilization, 20–25; environmental biasing and, 29–32; growth of towns and cities, 149; human nature and, 27–29; overview of, 20; population trends and, 148, 149, 150
agriculture: American farm productivity, 195–96; ancient climate change and, 31–32; corn, 175–76; cultural diffusion theory and, 26; efficient use of resources and, 198; possible origin of farms, 34; river flooding and, 32
AIDS, 133, 140, 153
air pollution, 177, 193, 207
alcohol, as a fuel, 175–76
Alexander the Great, 35–36
Alexandra (Empress of Russia), 69
Alhambra, 39
Al Jazeera, 6
alphabets, Semitic-Greek, 37–38
Alsace-Lorraine, 59, 60
America: European discovery of, 45, 46; industrialization in, 50; Spanish exploitation of, 46. *See also* Latin America; North America